LIFE BY THE LIFFEY
A Kaleidoscope of Dubliners

D0796931

Life by the Liffey

A *Kaleidoscope* of *Dubliners*

John O'Donovan

Gill and Macmillan

Published in Ireland by
Gilland Macmillan Ltd
Goldenbridge
Dublin 8
with associated companies in
Auckland, Dallas, Delhi, Hong Kong,
Johannesburg, Lagos, London, Manzini,
Melbourne, Nairobi, New York, Signapore,
Tokyo, Washington
© The Estate of the late John O'Donovan 1986
5 4 3 2 1
0 7171 1387 6
Print origination in Ireland by Wellset Ltd
Printed in Hong Kong.

All rights reserved. No part of this publication may be
copied, reproduced or transmitted in any form or by any
means, without permission of the publishers.

CONTENTS

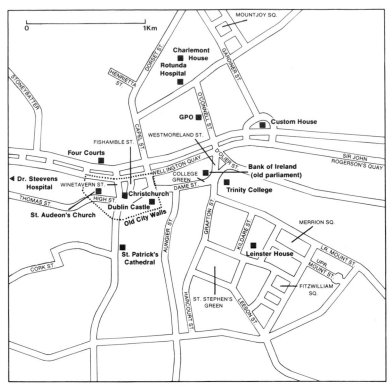

Dublin: city centre.

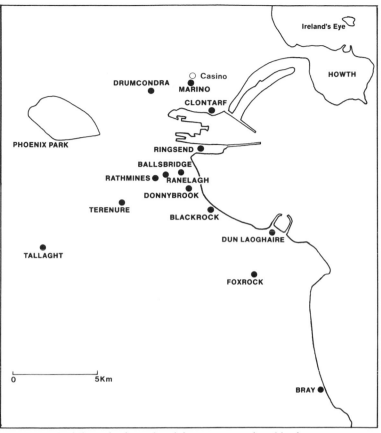

Dublin: suburbs and outlying areas mentioned in the text.

OVERTURE

DUBLIN has been embattled during most of its existence. Today many citizens would perceive the enemy as the mugger, the joyrider, the burglar, the drug pusher, the developer and the vandal whose depredations are encouraged by the absence of vigilant protection of property and the public interest. This kind of lawlessness is neither new nor unique to Dublin. It's the revival of an eighteenth- and nineteenth-century situation which has been brought about by much the same social conditions: too many people without jobs and without hope of them.

In its early years Dublin had to live with the constant threat of invasion by Danes and Scandinavians coming in from over the sea, and by the native Irish attacking by land. In later years there was always the uneasy wondering about when social unrest would once more erupt into an attempt at revolution, an uneasiness which was easily stampeded into panic during the Fenian era. (It's touch and go whether this situation might not recur today.)

Nevertheless, even when Fenianism was at its height, few thought that such revolutionary movements could enjoy more than brief success. Ireland was part of the British Empire, and the Empire could be depended upon to re-impose the rule of English law in the end. America had been the exception. But the general feeling about America was that the Empire was well rid of it. Reports on the American way of life made it clear that in no other country was morality more talked about and less observed in business, sex and politics — reports which were mightily reinforced by Dickens's writings about the New World. Obviously America was no place for a gentleman to live in.

But Ireland was. Always provided that the gentleman wasn't

1

too particular about what surrounded his own immediate surroundings. And Dublin was the most gentlemanly place in Ireland. Somebody in the eighteenth century adjudged it 'the second city of the Empire,' and long after the grain of truth in that statement had crumbled away, Dublin was still assuring puzzled visitors that they were now in The Second City.

No other city, said Dubliners, possessed so many splendid buildings, and they rattled off the familiar list like so many Hail Marys in a decade of the Rosary: the Custom House, the Four Courts, Trinity College, the Old Parliament House (made redundant by the Act of Union and re-employed as head office of the Bank of Ireland), the Rotunda, the General Post Office, Charlemont House, the Casino at Marino, The Lodge, the Castle, and that typical example of Irish *embarras de richesse*, two cathedrals of the same denomination.

In Dublin Castle, citizens would tell you, there was a large apartment, St Patrick's Hall, which was assuredly the largest and most magnificent in the British Isles, an opinion which used stagger incoming ducal viceroys to whom it would have appeared hardly larger that their own diningrooms at home. Visitors hearing of 'The Lodge' and asking what and where it was, were pitied for their ignorance. Didn't the whole world know that The Lodge was the Viceregal Lodge in the Park?

The Park??

Good heavens, man, the Phoenix Park, the largest park in the world. Look at Sackville (O'Connell) Street, the widest in Europe. The best English was spoken in Dublin. Dublin wit was celebrated. . . .

In a word, nineteenth-century Dublin hadn't yet grasped that it was only the least insignificant city in an island off an island off mainland Europe. Nor did it yet realize that it was a century behind the times in its appearance, and two in its ideas. But it did have the advantage of being cheap enough for persons of narrow means to cut a dash in.

Another advantage. Dublin had no patience with British hairsplitting about social classes, with their working class, lower middle class, middle class, upper middle class and so on. Dublin grandly simplified the matter: you were either a gentleman or you were not, although down the country, where people had little to do, they tended to go in for fine distinctions between gentry, mounted gentry, and half mounted gentry. (The term

2

squire wasn't much used, but tuppence-ha'penny was apt to call tuppence a squireen.)

Dublin was cheap for the usual reason. The bulk of the population was poor and the bulk of that bulk was destitute. In fact Dublin's attribute of having everything only in the superlative degree could be properly applied to its poor. They were amongst the poorest in Europe, their slums notoriously the worst of any European city. An English actor-satirist, Samuel Foote, raised a laugh by saying he hadn't known what London beggars did with their cast-off clothes until he saw Dublin beggars.

That was in the late eighteenth century when Dublin was relatively prosperous. In the nineteenth the vast increase in its population, without a corresponding increase in supportive local industry and commerce, had brought about a frightening deterioration in conditions for the poor. The finding of a human being, starved to skin and bone, lying dead in a doorway, was so commonplace that it hardly earned two lines in the newspaper. For him or her begging hadn't been enough, there was nothing for it but to die. The poorhouse was no real alternative. The Dublin poor well knew that to enter that place was to sentence yourself to death by cholera or some other dread fever.

The good news was that there was no servant problem. A cook could be had for £8 a year, a skivvy for less than half that. Families with incomes of around £100 a year could be domestically attended on a genteel scale. A moderately successful Dublin doctor, lawyer, or shopkeeper could live in a twenty-roomed town house and have a place in the country, both adequately staffed, and keep a carriage and pair, without making the neighbours wonder how the deuce he managed it. They knew. They were doing it themselves. Like for instance Samuel M'Comas. He kept a tailoring establishment in Dame Street, a castle in Dalkey on the Dublin coast, and a yacht in the bay.

Political corruption was a normal part of public life. The recognised way of becoming a judge was to manoeuvre yourself into parliament (easy if you knew enough influential College men to wangle a university seat for you), and then either lick boots or make a patriotic nuisance of yourself until a vacancy at the Fourt Courts enabled the government to get you out of their way. One barrister packed juries so zealously for the government that he was contemptuously named Pether the Packer. He was to end up Lord Chief Justice of Ireland, with, inevitably, a

3

mansion in the city, another in the outer suburbs, and an estate in the County Clare.

It wouldn't be true to say that all nineteenth-century Irish mitres were obtained as Swift alleged they had been in his day. He explained how the government appointed pious and learned divines to vacant Irish sees, but these worthies were waylaid on the journey to Ireland by highwaymen who stole their clothes and documents and got themselves consecrated. A nineteenth-century marquess with political muscle did get a younger brother made primate, who in turn arranged for the primacy to pass to a nephew, so that for the greater part of that century the Church of Ireland was ruled by a Beresford.

Rev. William Conyngham Plunket, grandson of a bigoted and time-serving Lord Chancellor of Ireland, and heir to the family barony, found it no hindrance in his progress towards a mitre that his father-in-law, Sir Benjamin Lee Guinness (of the brewery) restored St Patrick's Cathedral at his own expense. Sir Benjamin, the bustling little administrator of genius who set the brewery on the road to international prominence and the family to multimillionairedom, at one stroke earned himself a baronetcy, strengthened the Irish Church at a time of crisis brought about by Gladstone's 1869 disestablishment, and had his son-in-law promoted from a minor post in the cathedral chapter to the springboard to episcopacy. Not that Plunket disgraced his position. He was able, diplomatic, well liked and mildly controversial, endearing himself to the Mothers Union by raising his episcopal apron to show the ladies the he too wore one, and also that he had forgotten to adjust his dress before leaving.

Dublin's municipal corruption passed belief. The Corporation having annihilated countless thousands of children in the municipally controlled Foundling Hospital, went on to facilitate regular cholera epidemics by their treatment — or rather their non-treatment — of the city sewage. The Liffey was an open sewer, the streets, even in fashionable areas, were muddy cart tracks that became almost impassable after heavy rain. The city fathers weren't going to raise the rates on themselves (many being extensive property owners) in the cause of civic improvement. Besides, anyone with 6d ($2\frac{1}{2}$p) to spare needn't dirty his boots because he could have himself driven by horse cab from one end of the city to the other. Sixpence was the legal fare, and

4

though the cabby might picturesquely curse the passenger who forced him to get the last ounce out of the half-starved horse, little could be done about it.

Except in the newer suburbs squalor was to be found everywhere, even in mansions. Fastidious persons had to resign themselves to dust and grime. It came from open coal fires in inefficient hearths, from the unpaved unswept streets, from what would nowadays be an intolerable want of sanitation and personal hygiene that produced plagues of flies, bluebottles and cockroaches, and from the irredeemable sluttishness of servants. Thackeray, visiting Dublin in the summer of 1842, memorably sketched a window in the city's leading hotel, the Shelbourne, being propped open with a hearth brush because its cords and weights had long since gone out of commission.

But Thackeray was able to add that the tariff was more than reasonable. Bed and breakfast cost 6s 3d (32p), meals were lavish, wine unstinted. Such were Dublin's priorities. The insidious decline in standards in the once exclusive districts was hardly noticed. The grand houses, put up in spacious squares during the upsurge in national prosperity in the second half of the previous century, had been so handsomely and so durably furnished that after three quarters of a century they were by Dublin standards presentable. But carpets and hangings were seldom replaced when necessary, upholstery and fittings became shabby. Income went mainly on entertainment and the upkeep of wine cellar and carriage. It was not unknown for the mistresses of Merrion Square mansions, when ready money was scarce, to make ball dresses for themselves and their daughters out of curtains. (So, at any rate, alleges Percy Fitzgerald in his *Recollections of Dublin Castle and of Dublin Society.*) The beggar at the gate, telling the emerging gentleman that he didn't know where his next dinner was coming from, might well have got the reply: 'Neither do I.'

Of course these examples of shabby gentility don't make the complete picture. The country was burdened with an overmanned and elaborate public service which, Ireland being part of the United Kingdom, was salaried as of right on the English scale. In England these public servants would have been no more comfortably off. Ireland's lower cost of living put them in the highly prosperous class, and there were enough of them to support a Dublin street or two of expensive shops and, in the

5

1870s, to fill the dress circle and stalls of the new theatre, the Gaiety, which the enterprising Gunn brothers had built on the English model in South King Street (convenient to the fashionable squares) for the presentation of London successes by English touring companies.

For the only style that mattered in well-bred Dublin was the English style, the only fashion the London fashions, the only opinions those generated by Britain's imperial position. Dublin's clubs were modelled on London's, its literature came from Paternoster Row, its machinery, like the whole country's, from Coventry and Birmingham, its coal from British mines, and its tweeds, serges, silks and satins, its chinaware and pottery, its knives and forks were likewise of English provenance. The very guns and surgical knives used by Irish political assassins had to be imported from England, hidden in the petticoats of sympathetic girl friends. Well-bred Dublin, derided by the nationalists as *shoneens* and West Britons, regarded itself as an honourable part of the British connection.

But there were limits. If Dublin aped London manners it drew back from London morals. Whoring was confined strictly to the professional practitioners and done only in the recognised districts. Otherwise Irish womanhood remained chaste as a matter of course, and although Dublin bandinage was sometimes broader than London's, gallantry stopped at words, deeds being puritanically inhibited. The Irishwoman's knowledge and experience of the sex repertoire, in so far as can be judged in such a matter, was elementary. For when a viceroy, Lord Houghton, allegedly invited the well-built wife of a Lord Mayor of Dublin to retire with him to a quiet corner of The Lodge to birch his buttocks for him, the lady, mystified by what she regarded as a reversal of the natural procedure, consulted intimate friends as to what on earth his Excellency could really have meant. 'And his Ex.', she said, deepening the mystery for the Dublin ladies, 'hadn't any signs of drink on him either.'

If the story was widely told then this may have been owing in some measure to 'Haughty Houghton's' unpopularity with the nationalists, they being eager to publicise examples of Saxon decadence.

Dublin papers in the 1880s had no occasion to report native divorce cases like the Campbell case in London. *The Times* impassively recorded how Lady Colin Campbell, married off to a son of the Duke of Argyll, who was disabled by syphilis (and a homosexual into the bargain), dispensed the most lavish hospitality in her drawingroom of an afternoon to a succession of gentlemen callers. The butler's evidence, which gave rise to the tag about What the Butler Saw, included a graphic description of how, peeping through the keyhole, he saw her ladyship sprawled on the sofa, legs in the air, while the Chief of the London Fire Brigade tried to extinguish her recurrent fire.

Dublin professed shock when it read these reports, dutifully retailed in the local papers. The shock wasn't merely at such goings-on in English society but at realising that Lady Colin Campbell was originally a Miss Blood from the Co. Clare, and the ardent fireman none other than Captain Eyre Massey Shaw, originally from the ironically named Monkstown in Co. Cork. (He was a cousin of George Bernard Shaw.)

However it hardly mattered what Irish men and women got up to in pagan England. The important thing was that they should behave properly in Christian Ireland. In Christian Dublin apparent improprieties were generally found to have quite innocent explanations. For example, the Anglican arch-bishop, Richard Chenevix Trench, palpated the knee of the young lady sitting beside him at dinner, mentioning after a while that he had been rubbing his knee for some time but could feel nothing. His clergy soothed the fears of their parishioners by explaining that his Grace was notoriously absentminded, so that this apostolic laying on of hands was perfectly harmless.

Visitors to the city felt that the beggars need not have been quite so dirty, quite so ragged, quite so servile. Readers of Swift remembered how the dean himself had complained on the same score. To the owner of a pair of filthy claws held out to him for alms he said that soap and water weren't so scarce as to put clean hands out of the question even for the poor. As for the servility, Dubliners knew that in many cases this was the thin covering of hatred. The poor, not only in Dublin but all over the country, believed that their poverty and the prosperity of others were not accidents of birth or circumstances but the direct consequence of English rule. The small shopkeeper, living as much from hand to mouth as most of his customers, believed that if only the English could be driven out of Ireland the world would beat a path to his counter. The back street tailor knew it was the English presence alone which prevented more people from ordering suits from

7

him at treble the ordinary price. The bootmaker declared he wouldn't be able to cope with the flow of custom if only the English were gone, and the staymaker echoed the words. The Dublin born composer Charles Villiers Stanford, who as a Cambridge professor influenced three generations of British composers for better and for worse, put the case witheringly: 'If only we had home rule our symphonies would be as good as Beethoven's.'

The widespread discontent amongst the have-nots provided ever fertile ground for the propaganda of sedition, crime (committed from the highest motives of course) and assassination. The appeals to patriotic sentiment from earnest young idealists went down well, even when the same few themes were hammered out week after week after week in *The Nation*. But the rancid rhetoric of the political adventurers and self promoters went down better. It must have been unnerving for masters and mistresses to drive past a street corner meeting and notice their footman and chambermaid, all smiles and dimples when on duty, and the shop assistants who had been so helpful and obsequious that afternoon, now screeching approval of calls to have the Saxon tyrant seethed in his own blood. Upper crust Dublin became very jittery at rumours that yet another rebellion was brewing. Jitteriness had caused William Magee, one of Dublin's less amusing archbishops, to order new churches to be constructed like fortresses, with narrow lancet windows set high in the walls, the doors narrow as well, the more easily to make these houses of God refuges for Protestants menaced by ravening hordes of emancipated Roman Catholics.

Emancipation came and went, as did Archbishop Magee, but the Catholics remained quiet and churches continued to be used only for divine service. However other factors altered the general situation. The Great Famine, which starved the peasantry to death or to America in coffin ships, reduced the landlords' income accordingly. Retrenchment helped some to survive. Others were irretrievably edged towards bankruptcy. Less money was spent in Dublin, whose poor, during that awful winter of 1847, pleaded so piteously for scraps that the Lord Lieutenant, the Earl of Bessborough, a major landowner in Co. Kilkenny, was moved to respond. He ordered the Castle cook to send out a beef bone for the communal stockpot.

Not long afterwards he dropped dead. As his body was being

8

ceremonially borne from the Castle, a vengeful crowd delivered their obituary. They carried in the funeral procession a bone dangling from a pole.

Small wonder that the following year, 1848, fifty years after the United Irishmen's uprising had been bloodily suppressed, the revolutionary movement which swept across Europe caused ripples in Ireland. At the time these seemed no more than very minor, even ludicrous, disturbances of the public peace which soon died away. But they gave rise to another movement, Fenianism, which idealistically and politically offered little more than the same mixture as before. But because its first leader happened to have a talent for organising and a genius for propaganda, Fenianism seized the nation's imagination as no other revolutionary movement had done before in Ireland, moulding life and opinion in the country and its capital not only until the formation of the Free State in 1922 but in some vital respects to the present day.

9

1

EARLY DAYS

1

FROM the earliest times the River Liffey was noted for its muddy waters, causing the city to be named Blackpool, in Gaelic *Dubh Linn*. This was Englished as Dublin, a version soon superseding the clumsy name of Town of the Ford of the Hurdles.

The relentless flow of people from the provinces into the capital is a fact of life in all countries. Dublin was no different in this respect. But the flow may have had for some people the added attraction of forbidden fruit because for a long time Dublin, being largely a foreigners' settlement, was a Forbidden City to the native Irish. After the English took over in the twelfth century the Irish were still excluded. The word went out: 'No Irish man nor men with beards above the mouth to be lodged within the wall of the city of Dublin,' and by parliamentary decree an Englishman 'shall have no hairs on his upper lip — so that the said lip shall be at least shaven every fortnight.'

The city began to be effectively enclosed by walls after Henry II made his favourite son, John ('Lack-land'), Lord of Ireland. In 1204 John, now King of England, ordered a castle to be built in Dublin and walls put up around the city. As a result, an area approximately equal to the modern St Stephen's Green was enclosed with walls whose infirmity even then emphasised the limitations of the Corporation's craftsmanship. To keep these walls standing, the Dublin ratepayers of the thirteenth and subsequent centuries groaned under a heavy financial burden. The items taxed indicate the variety of commodities upon which early Dublin commerce was founded. The list includes wheat, flour, wine, honey, hides, wood, iron, herrings, oxen, cows, horses, sheep, goats, pigs, boars, horseshoes, tallow, butter, spice, wax, alum, millstones, linen, canvas, lead, beans, kitchenware.

The eagerness of the native Irish to get into Dublin to enjoy urban life, to pursue a commercial career, or at least get a job with the Corporation, caused Dubliners to adopt strong measures to keep them out. For their own convenience the Dubliners had to have several gates in their walls. Stanihurst in 1577 names eight: 'White friers, Saint Kevin his Gate, Hogs Gate, Dammes Gate, Paule Gate, Newgate, Winetavern Gate, Saint Audoen his Gate, hard by the Church, going down by the Cooke Streete.' But a day and night watch was kept at the gates and on their tops, as well as on the walls and towers. The watchers were instructed to keep an eye on any Irishman who came to the city and to bring him before the mayor if he had an immigrant air about him. Truly would he be the Mayoman of the Year who could get through any Dublin gate with the medieval equivalent of a suitcase or other piece of luggage suggesting a protracted stay.

The mayor for his part was commanded to have the city searched three times a week for 'masterless' persons — in other words, the unemployed — who would probably have experienced a *mauvais quart d'heure* before being run out of town into the swamp that later became O'Connell Street. Social welfare was a concept far beyond the intellectual or spiritual grasp of a medieval Dublin mayor, as indeed it has proved to be beyond that of some of his twentieth-century successors.

So, the city having been cleared of undesirables (unestablished ones at any rate), the gates were closed at sunset after the customary warning drum beat and tolling of the bell of St Audoen's. Responsibility for closing the gate lay with the alderman of the ward in which it stood, and the keys had to be carried by him to the mayor. The night watch was kept by sentinels at fixed stations, and by patrols. An hourly inspection was carried out by a captain attended by armed guards. As well as all this, assembly points were specified at which all citizens in the vicinity were to gather fully armed on hearing any alarm or sudden cry. Clearly the protection afforded by the Corporation's walls didn't enjoy the total confidence of those within.

Eternal vigilance was necessary. Dubliners were aware that the eyes of adventurous chieftains in all parts of the island were fixed hungrily on their city. They therefore executed what would now be called pre-emptive strikes, sallying forth into the

11

territories of the native chieftains to display their strength but without fighting if they could help it. They had of course an old score to settle with the O'Byrnes and O'Tooles of the Dublin and Wicklow mountains. On Easter Monday 1209, citizens and their families had ventured out to Cullen's Wood (Ranelagh) for a holiday outing. The mountainy men, seeing the Dubliners now at their mercy, crept down the hillside, pounced on the revellers and slaughtered five hundred of them.

For centuries afterwards that Easter Monday was known as Black Monday and the scene of the slaughter the 'Bloody Fields'. The city could ill afford to lose five hundred inhabitants, so a new colony had to be sent in from Bristol, and the custom was begun of citizens ceremonially marching out to the Bloody Fields fully armed and with banners flying. Almost exactly two hundred years later, in 1406, the Wicklow men again tried conclusions with the Dubliners. This time the result was a row of Wicklow heads on spikes around the city walls.

The citizens had other problems to contend with. Plague and pestilence annihilated them by the hundred: it was the price the city had to pay for almost total abstinence from hygiene and sanitation. Not that the Corporation was standing idly by. If they failed to keep the city safely clean they at least acted to propitiate the gods of pestilence. After a visitation of typhus, cholera, or whatever, the surviving householders were required to burn a faggot outside their doors three evenings a week: Mondays, Wednesdays and Saturdays. The city fathers believed that the smoke would purify the air.

Fire was another constant hazard, most of the houses being of wood and thatched. But this was a hazard shared by virtually every other conurbation of the time, and Dublin, though it suffered many damaging outbreaks, seems to have escaped holocausts like the great Fire of London. However, the unsturdiness of its buildings made it very vulnerable to storms and floods. We read that as far back as 1313 a bridge at Ballybough was swept away by floods, whilst the steeple of Christchurch Cathedral was blown down three years later. In December 1338 a frost began which lasted until the following February, during which time the Liffey was so thickly frozen that people played football and lit fires on the ice.

The river is alleged to have performed in 1452 the remarkable feat of going completely dry for two minutes, but a more credible event is the 'violent tempest' a few years later which blew in the east window of Christchurch. The chroniclers record that in 1534 an earthquake was distinctly felt in the city, a thing which will be readily believed by those citizens who felt the ground rocking beneath them some 450 years later.

Christchurch cathedral seems to have escaped significant damage in the big gale of 1668, but the steeple of St Audoen's, a few yards away, was blown down. Two years later, in consequence of 'a great storm at new moon', the Liffey overflowed into what is now Pearse Street, flooding the grounds of Trinity College. In 1716 and in 1724 occurred two other memorable storms which wrecked many houses, and the winter of 1741-42 was so severe that it caused widespread unemployment. Relief works had to be started to assist starving tradesmen, including the building of various 'follies,' two of the best known in the Dublin area being the obelisks at Stillorgan and on the top of Killiney Hill.

The Liffey misbehaved itself again in January 1792, flooding the area between Sir John Rogerson's Quay and Ringsend after part of the South Wall had given way, and leaving Ringsend inaccessible from the city except by boat. The papers reported that 'His Grace the Duke of Leinster went on a sea party, and after shooting the breach in the south wall, sailed over the low ground in the south lots and landed safely at Merrion Square.'

The later embankment of the Liffey has kept the river more or less in its place, although it again showed its spirit on 6 January 1839, celebrating the 'Night of the Big Wind' by overflowing the quay walls in several places. The Dodder went on the spree too, and up to recent years used regularly sweep away stretches of its retaining walls at Orwell Road, Rathgar, until the authorities finally tamed its waters with massive structures of reinforced concrete.

But if the records are to be believed, Dublin's worst ever bout of bad weather occurred in 1739 when, beginning on 29 December, severe frost refrigerated the city until the 8 February following. It was a repeat performance of the episode of four centuries before, the Liffey being again frozen over and Dubliners playing games on the ice. This time however the Corporation sent along labourers to hack a passage out for the coal boats.

It wasn't all jollity. That winter several Dubliners were frozen to death in the streets, and the three Lord Justices, headed by

13

Hugh Boulter, Archbishop of Armagh, called out the military to chase away some men and women who were cutting down a few trees in the Phoenix Park in a desperate attempt to get the means to keep warm.

2

Few of the poor in medieval Dublin need have gone hungry when so much potential food was trotting around the streets and the pastures outside the walls. The number of pigs roaming the streets was such a nuisance that the city bailiffs were ordered to kill them with pikes and stack the carcases on carts. There doesn't seem to have been much to prevent a needy citizen lassooing a passing animal and saving the bailiffs a job. If tired of bacon and pork chops, he need only take a discreet midnight ramble to St Stephen's Green, which was a sheepwalk. My guess is that the needy citizen was in trouble only when old age and the decay of his physical faculties enabled the sheep and the pigs to move faster than he could. Survival would then depend upon how successful he had been in imbuing his children with a sense of responsibility for providing for aged parents, and upon how charitable the monks of St Mary's Abbey really were.

Since the embanked River Liffey was easily accessible to all citizens, it might be presumed that fish were freely available. The twelfth-century chronicler, Gerald of Wales, had commented on the abundance of fish on all Irish coasts, lakes and rivers. But there appears to have been considerable racketeering in fish from the earliest times, so that if you couldn't loot the river on your own account you had to resign yourself to be looted by the fishmonger. The big fish centre in medieval Dublin was indicated by the name: Fishamble Street. In 1356 the government ordered the marketing of fish to be confined to the shambles, an ordinance which smoothed for fishmongers the path to succulent profits. The marketing methods of the fourteenth and fifteenth centuries had that classic simplicity which has continued through the ages. In the middle of the week the fishmongers bought up every catch landed between Holmpatrick and the city and made everyone pay through the nose for the obligatory Friday fish dinner.

The practice was called forestalling, and public anger forced the government to set up a commission of four to investigate the grievance and remedy it. The four worthies were to keep an eye on things at the Co. Dublin harbours, stop the buying up of all catches by the racketeers, and ensure that all fish landed were forwarded to the official market for sale to the public. The commissioners were also empowered to search the houses of persons suspected of racketeering, and to jail anyone with more fish in the kitchen than could reasonably be required for Friday's dinner.

The supply of meat doesn't appear to have raised many problems of this kind. All the evidence points to the consumption of great quantities of wine and beer as a matter of course, with home brewing being as common as home baking. The twelfth-century biographer of St Laurence O'Toole, Archbishop of Dublin, records that the saint used to regale his guests with various wines. These may have come from the wine merchants whose widespread presence in the street adjoining Christchurch Cathedral caused it to be named Winetavern Street, a name surviving to the present day.

The import and export of wines seem to have formed one of the major trades of old Dublin, although considerably less must have been exported than was imported judging by such statistics of drinking as we have. Richard Stanyhurst (1547-1618), son of a Recorder of Dublin, who contributed a *Description of Ireland* to Holinshed's *Chronicles,* tells us that Patrick Sarsfield, mayor in 1554 and ancestor of *the* Sarsfield, claimed that during his year of office his household consumption of claret was twenty tuns, over and above white wine, sack, malvoisie, muscatel, and so on. Dublin's mayoral hospitality was praised as second only to London's.

A few years later a Dublin Castle official reported that the taverns sold Spanish and French wines, and that when the native Irish

> come to any market towne to sell a cow or a horse, they never returne home till they have drunke the price in Spanish wine (which they call the king of Spaine's daughter), or in Irish Usqueboagh.

If Barnaby Rich (c. 1540-1620) is to be believed, the 'whole profit' of old Dublin stood upon

> ale-houses and the selling of ale . . . there are whole streates

15

of tavernes and it is as rare a thing to finde a house in Dublin without a taverne, as to find a taverne without a strumpet.

Barnaby (or Barnabe) Rich was a prolific English pamphleteer, romance-writer and soldier whose military service included a spell in Ireland. He alleges that almost every woman in Dublin brewed ale for sale to the public, the most active brewers being the wives of the city aldermen. Since he adds that any Dublin woman whose credit 'will serve to borowe a pan and to buy but a mesure of mault in the market, setts up brewing,' one wonders where the customers came from, especially as the ladies didn't sell cheaply. According to Barnaby they were able to buy their 'mault' at half the London price 'but sold at double the rate they doe in London'. Seeing that so many aldermanic wives were in the business it's hardly surprising that 'the mayor and his brethern are the willinger to wink at the overcharging'.

Barnaby used the term tavern ironically, for he had noted the Irish fondness for inflated language whereby every pedlar became a merchant and every ale house a tavern.

> Then they have a number of young ydle huswives, that are both verie loathsome, filthie and abominable, both in life and manners, and these they call taverne keepers, the most of them knowne harlots; these doe take in both ale and beere by the barrell from those that do brue, and they sell it forthe againe by the potte, after twoe pence for a wine quart.

Nor was Barnaby favourably impressed by the quality of the brew, because, as he says, he had been so long amongst

> these filthy ale houses, that my head beginnes to grow idle, and it is no wonder, for the very remembrance of that hogge's wash which they use to sell for i j.d (twopence) the wine quart, is able to distemper any man's brains and as it is neither good nor wholesome, so it is unfit for any man's drinking, but for common drunkards.

By the 1660s there were no fewer than ninety-one public breweries serving Dublin, and some 1,180 pubs retailing. As the population was reckoned to be 4,000 families the proportion was about one pub to every three families.

16

3

It was a woman, Lady Morgan (born Sydney Owenson), some-
time a well-known Irish novelist, who penned its most enduring
label on Dublin. Dear, old, and dirty remain apt to the ear.
Dublin, still dear in the financial sense if not in the other, is old
enough to have a character to be destroyed by insensitive
development, and in spite of anti-litter legislation is dirty by
comparison with other European capitals though not by comparison with its former self.

Clean cities are of course a recent development in the civilised
world. Sanitation, personal hygiene to the point of frequent
bathing and changes of linen, together with the regular vacuum
cleaning of one's home, not to mention the cleaning and main-
tenance of streets and bridges, requires elaborate and costly
back-up services, involving reservoirs, sewage disposal schemes,
power stations and the labour force needed to work them.
Without such services the standard of personal and public
hygiene falls catastrophically. Dublin dirt in the old days was
therefore inevitable; the difference between it and the dirt of
London, Paris, Rome, and other capitals can only have been
one of degree. What drew down Lady Morgan's amused
comment must have been the avoidable personal dirt of the
inhabitants even more than the unavoidable dirt of their
surroundings. She was neither the first nor the last to remark on
Irish dirt. The truth seems to be that by present day standards of
sanitation and hygiene all medieval cities and their inhabitants
must have been repulsive.

In 1766 the churchwardens of St Werburgh's were obliged to
pass a resolution forbidding any seat in the church to be lined or
hung with any kind of cloth, silk, or stuff, to prevent as much as
possible any lodgment of vermin. This apparently was the great
nuisance complained of in neighbouring churches. But then
even London streets had their

> Sweepings from butcher's stalls, dung, guts, and blood,
> Drown'd puppies, stinking sprats, all drench'd in mud

so that the London gentleman, unless he travelled everywhere
by carriage or sedan chair, had to have his shoes cleaned three or
four times a day. John Gay in his *Trivia* (1716) tells how

> The black youths at chosen stands rejoice,
> And 'clean your shoes' resounds from ev'ry voice.

17

More than your shoes could be soiled unless you were very vigilant.

> Ye walkers, too, that youthful colours wear,
> Three sullying trades avoid with equal care;
> The little chimney-sweeper skulks along
> And marks with sooty stain the heedless throng...
> The chandler's basket, on his shoulder borne,
> With tallow spots thy coat; resign the way
> To shun the surly butcher's greasy tray.

Conditions in the home, even in the homes of the upper class, were just as bad as in the street, as we can deduce from Swift's ironical *Directions to Servants*, in which he pretends to recommend to servants the practices he himself found most objectionable. It seems that in those days ladies did not powder their noses or spend pennies but 'stepped into the garden to pluck a rose.' The directions for the housemaid tells us, however, that some ladies preferred to keep

> An odious implement, sometimes in the bed-chamber, itself, or at least in a dark closet adjoining, which they make use of to ease their worst necessities; and you are the usual carriers away of the pan, which maketh not only the chamber, but even their clothes, offensive to all who come near.

The housemaid was recommended to discourage the practice by carrying the pan

> openly down the great stairs, and in the presence of the footman; and, if anybody knocks, to open the street-door, while you have the vessel filled in your hands.

Since there was no sewerage system as we know it, the contents of the pan would have been disposed of either in a neighbourhood cesspit, or, as seems to have been the more common practice in Dublin, in the street gutter outside the house. Clearance would be left to the operation of the city showers or to the occasional ministrations of an official scavenger, appointed by the Corporation who dumped his (or her) loads just a little distance away. The insertion of the 'her' in the previous sentence is necessary because the most notable city scavenger in the old days was Katherine Strong(e), a widow whom another marriage turned into Katherine White, although she has descended in Dublin lore as Kate Strong.

Her notability was founded not on the excellence of her scavenging but on her efficiency in fleecing everyone she could on the strength of her self-promulgated regulations.

By the terms of her appointment she was granted certain market tolls, chiefly at the fish markets, in return for employing six men with six horses and carts to keep the streets clean, collect domestic refuse and dump it well outside the city. Kate ordained that two men would be enough for the work, especially as she wasn't dumping the rubbish 'beyond Oxmantown Green' as required. In 1632 she was reported for dumping rubbish 'which she gathereth in the easte parte of this citty' on the river bank unpleasantly close to Mr George Baddely's garden in Dame Street,

> by which meanes the river is soe stopt, that a small gabbart cannot come to the Key with her loadinge . . .

The Corporation ordered the Dame Street aldermen and constables to detain any carter found dumping in any spot mentioned in Mr Baddely's petition, the carter not to be freed until a fine of two shillings had been paid. Kate's spirited response seems to have been to cut down the collection of rubbish and increase her collection of tolls. In 1634 the complaint was that she and her henchmen James Bellewe and John Butcher had extorted so much at the fish market that 'the poore are oppressed much'. The dealers petitioned the Corporation to get Kate off their backs and to make clear just what she was entitled to exact.

But the Corporation seems to have been unable to control Kate because the Mayor, Sir James Carroll, now formally complained to the highest authority in the land, the Lord Deputy, about her. Not only was she taking whatever amount of fish she pleased from the fish market as a toll, but she and her henchmen went to the various city gates and extorted quantities of butter, eggs, cheese, wool, fish, roots, and cabbage from the producers before she would let them enter the city to sell what was left.

As for street cleaning, this was now confined to sweeping 'sparingly' the short stretches of highway between the Castle, the mayor's house and Christchurch Cathedral to facilitate these dignitaries should they happen to be going to divine service. The other citizens were left to put up with the 'foul and offensive' streets.

19

It was not Kate who found herself in hot water, however, but the mayor. The following year he was brought before the Lord Deputy he had memorialised about her, charged with setting a rate of sixteen shillings a ton on coal that had been imported at eight shillings, and selling coal at even higher rates for his private profit. Asked what excuse he could offer, he pleaded ignorance of any regulation which prevented him from doing this in his capacity as Clerk of the Market. The plea was contemptuously rejected. Sir James was removed from the office of mayor, debarred from holding public office in future, fined £1,000 and jailed.

The indomitable Kate continued her depredations unhindered until at least 1640, the odd fact emerging that her successor was declared to be even worse than she had been.

Inevitably part of the very centre of the old city became a dump of sorts. Because of this ground levels rose over the years. Excavations in the 1970s in the area around Christchurch Cathedral, the heart of the old city, uncovered so many layers of refuse over the remains of Viking dwellings, that the hill upon which the cathedral stands is clearly as much man-made as the cathedral itself.

The sociological information yielded by these excavations, and the number and variety of the homely objects turned up, have modified the view that the Dublin story doesn't become interesting to the layman until the sixteenth century, when we have the first of the gossipy travellers' accounts of the life style of the inhabitants. The discovery in the dump of the remains of medieval combs, shoes, leather jerkins, pots, pans and goblets is a reminder that the daily life of the ancient Dubliner must have been in many respects like that of the modern one.

2

DIVES AND LAZARUS

1

IT'S a fair deduction that in old Dublin enough crumbs and drops fell from the table of Dives to keep life in Lazarus. As the years went on, both classes increased in numbers, but the latter far outstripped the former and Lazarus became Dublin's most notorious social problem.

It's to be doubted whether Dublin's poor experienced the full horrors of their condition until the population began its steady increase in the eighteenth century. By then the city was no longer walled and guarded. Ingress and egress were uncontrolled, making it easy for the capital to be the Mecca of the nation's poor and hungry. In earlier times the controls of the number of inhabitants necessarily involved control of the number of the poor, so that the social problem of poverty could be 'contained'. The abandonment of controls meant that the small amount of relief had to be spread increasingly thinly.

Relief was mainly a matter of private benevolence, for the official bodies largely ignored their responsibilities in the matter, the Corporation of Dublin in particular. The Corporation, always an iniquitous body, had its crimes against humanity blazoned to the world when national registration of births, marriages and deaths, introduced into Britain in 1837, was extended to Ireland in 1864. The returns of the Registrar-General soon proved statistically that in every aspect of mortality Dublin had the worst record in these islands, the high death rates being caused by the pestiferous condition into which the city had been let fall by its official guardians. Augustine Birrell, a Chief Secretary in Edwardian times, wasn't the only holder of that office to be unable even to mention Dublin Corporation without having to delete expletives.

The city fathers had of course inherited a big problem. Until

21

1838 the poor in Ireland were to a great extent left to the charity of private individuals, the really effectual English statutes for relieving poverty not applying here. Thus the spirit if not the letter of a statute of Edward III could flourish in Ireland's official circles long after it had been superseded in England and Wales: that no one should give alms to a beggar able to work.*

By common law the poor had to be sustained by 'parsons, rectors of the church, and parishioners, so that none should die for default of sustenance'. But it wasn't until 1535 that the first really effective relief measure was enacted, a benevolence owed to Good King Henry VIII (as his subjects regarded him). Sixty-six years later his daughter Elizabeth I strengthened the 1535 enactment by providing overseers to ensure that the parishes fulfilled their statutory obligations, thus creating the beginning of Poor Law Relief as we know it, with its efflorescence into social welfare.

In Ireland parish poorhouses existed more to comply with common law than for genuine care of the needy. Only in 1838 was a measure of England's primitive social welfare extended to this country. The achievement was that of Queen Victoria's first prime minister, Lord Melbourne, who ten years earlier had been Irish Chief Secretary and therefore knew the score. It's worth noting that Ireland's first Poor Law was opposed by Irish M.P.s including William Smith O'Brien and Daniel O'Connell, a member of Dublin Corporation.

In obedience to the new legislation, workhouses were built throughout the country, their design being forbiddingly institutional, their furnishing rigorously spartan. But with all their faults they came not a moment too soon, being just in time to cope in so far as they were able with the effects of the Great Famine.

Meanwhile the workhouses afforded excuses to diminish private charity. Householders were now paying a poor rate: why should they pay double by disbursing personal alms? In practice, of course, the ordinary decent person didn't pause to consider the scanty benefits of the Poor Law when encountering an obviously starving woman with a famished child at her breast. To that extent benevolence continued, for you can't make people heartless by Act of Parliament. History tells of

*It was Edward III who also provided the treason statute by which Robert Emmet, Roger Casement, and a host of other Irish activists were hanged.

22

many an Irish landlord who ventured to the brink of bankruptcy in his efforts to hold back from the grave the Famine victims of his neighbourhood.

The situation seems to have been that even during the Famine people were prepared to suffer almost any extreme of hardship before submitting to the final humiliation of 'going on the parish'. During the winter of 1846-7 in Dublin Dr Lombe Atthill, later to become Master of the Rotunda Hospital, worked without pay for a charitable institution called the Fleet Street Dispensary which had been established to provide medical attention for the sick poor in their own homes. His district included the low-lying slums on the banks of the Liffey.

> One day I received a ticket directing me to visit a woman in one of these streets, not of the worst class. Calling at the address given, I was told that the patient lived in the 'kitchen' and as there was no communication between the house proper and the so-called kitchen I had to go out of the front door and down into the area to gain entrance. There I found the woman in a veritable cellar, into which neither air nor light could enter, save through the door. Her case was one of typhus fever, so I gave her an order for admission to the fever hospital.
>
> Before leaving I was asked to see another patient in the 'back room,' which I did. As it was pitch dark there, they lit a candle. Both these rooms were below high-water mark of the river, which was but a few yards distant. The outer cellar was bad enough, but the back one was frightful. There was neither window nor fireplace in it. The walls, which were wholly below the level of the ground, had never been plastered; down them trickled little streams of water, the floor was saturated with damp, the air foul, while on a kind of bed raised a few inches from the floor lay a girl ill with small-pox. . . .

Another of his experiences at that time almost passes belief. He was sent to visit a woman in a house in a lane.

> It was late on a winter day, and twilight. Arrived at the house I pushed the outer door in, and knocked on that of the first room I came to. Hearing no answer, I opened it and asked, 'Is there anyone here?' The room was pitch dark. I

could see nothing, but a voice from the far corner said, 'Yes.' Asking was she Mrs — —, 'Yes,' again came the reply. So I crept cautiously in the direction from whence the voice came. I could not see the patient, but, stooping down, felt the outline of a human form stretched on a little straw in the corner. There was no fire, no candle in the room, and as far as I could judge not a scrap of furniture. I asked her to raise her hand, and I felt the pulse; it was that of fever. I told her to put out her tongue, and, touching it, felt it as dry as a coarse file. I knew that it must be a case of typhus — alone, friendless, untended, without light, without fire, without food. Such was the daily experience of the physician. The only chance was to get such removed quickly to the 'fever sheds' erected outside the city, for the hospitals in the city were filled to excess.

Atthill adds that not only the sick poor succumbed but the doctors who attended them.

2

Dublin Corporation could hardly claim to be unaware that such conditions existed in the city. Visitors to Dublin reported that its poorer quarters were by no means hidden away, that you couldn't walk half a mile from the mansions of Dives without finding yourself in some foetid slum.

Rev. James Whitelaw, one of the compilers of a massive history and survey of Dublin published in 1818, confessed that he himself couldn't remain more than a few moments at a time in the lairs of the poor without having to go outside to draw a few mouthfuls of street air, itself hardly salubrious. Significantly he added that the inhabitants seemed unaware of the stenches, indeed seemed to find them 'congenial'. Which indicates that pity must often be wasted on those who live in the midst of nastiness. The truth is, the number of people who can voluntarily live in what appear to be conditions frightful to those with sensitive noses and ears and eyes, is much greater than is generally believed. As a young man I was invited to tea by a middle-class family, the occupants of an official residence attached to a Co. Dublin institution. The refreshment was served in the kitchen, the floor of which was encrusted with children's excrement, with a corner given over to a horribly stained enamel bucket used as a urinal to save the family going upstairs. The condition of my hostess's dress was hardly to be described since neither it nor its wearer appeared to have been washed for some years.

Yet this was the home of a man receiving a handsome salary as a public servant, together with many perks. He lived quite contentedly in this self-made slum, and I can certify that never have I known a happier or more carefree family.

Go into a Dublin pub lounge, overcrowded, noisy, smoky, dark, airless, and the grinning faces indicate that whatever the personal troubles and afflictions of the company, they aren't bothered by the foul atmosphere. Add to this that the Irish as a nation notoriously have no passion for ablution or for maintaining high standards of hygiene in their immediate surroundings. Add again that human beings have surprising powers of adapting to unfavourable circumstances and accommodating their needs to what is available. The conclusion must be that the sufferings of Dubliners during the classical period of the city's slums, when they had never known any other way of existing, may have been magnified by the fastidious. Victorian photographers picture for us the smiling happy faces of three-quarters starved ragged barefoot slum children. The smiles are to all appearances unforced.

What the poor really suffered was from winter's icy cold, from a perpetually unsatisfied appetite, and the ills attending these conditions.

Just what the wife and family of an unemployed Dublin workman lived on in the nineteenth century, we can only guess at. The poor kept no documentary record of their dietary. Social observers and charity visitors talk of a thin slice of dry bread per person, washed down with a mug of watery tea or cocoa, for breakfast, with the same in the evening. Occasionally there might be a herring or two to be divided amongst the whole family. And this was the diet of the poor, day after day, week after week.

Where the destitute got the few pennies to buy those slices of bread and occasional herrings is another challenge to the imagination. Was it from thieving, begging, running messages and doing odd jobs for the local shopkeeper? Was it from going out to scrub floors, wash clothes, sweep paths, help empty the cesspits of those who could afford them? Was it from selling bunches of flowers or heads of cabbage or boxes of matches? We know that in severe weather or in times of great distress, committees were set up to distribute free broth and small pieces of bread. We know that other committees shared out cast-off clothing and footwear. We know that relief societies existed by the score from whom the poor learned that mercy often droppeth from heaven with the gentleness of outsize hailstones and that the sip of eleemosynary soup had to be earned by standing there to be hosed down with texts of Holy Writ by the dog collared of all denominations. Much resentment, which had to be hidden, was generated by zealots who used their hearers' empty bellies as a theological argument for abandoning the faith of their fathers — or more accurately that of their mothers.

But wherever the pennies of the poor came from they were seldom enough to ward off the diseases that come from malnutrition, exposure, and the extremes of insanitary conditions. We are told that many of the slum houses contained sixty and more inhabitants. Most of these must have urinated and defecated in the back yard, or in vessels that were emptied into that yard, so that the sixty people were living over a cesspit. Even the houses of the better off contributed to the disease bomb, being fitted with drainage systems which emptied the effluent into the Liffey, which became an open sewer for the whole course of its journey through the city.

In the circumstances the wonder is not that Dublin held the British record for high mortality but that the entire city wasn't wiped out by cholera and typhus.

Yet here again one must pause to wonder whether faulty sanitation is quite the deadly evil the sanitation industry accuse it of being. The Prince Consort's death from typhoid in 1861 in Windsor Castle was attributed by the doctors to the castle's bad drains, and by Queen Victoria to the moral shock suffered by Albert the Good on discovering that the sweet mystery of life had been found by their teenage son in the arms of Miss Nellie Clifden in the Curragh Camp.

We are amused by Victoria's choice of superstition to believe in, and nod approvingly at the doctors'. But since the castle's bad drains left the rest of the royal family and their household unscathed, establishing that the castle's mortality rate from typhoid fever at that time was less than one-tenth of one per cent, you'd wonder whether Victoria's diagnosis mightn't have been nearer the truth after all.

3

Dives tended to make a cholesterolic banquet of each of the day's four meals. Mrs Mary Delany, the Englishwoman who was nursing mother to all Dublin gossip columnists, notes that at one dinner she was invited to in 1744 there was no dessert and only two courses.

It does sound rather frugal until you learn that the first course included turkey's endive, boiled neck of mutton, greens, soup, plum pudding, roast loin of veal and venison pasty. The second course brought partridge, sweetbreads, collared pig, creamed apple tarts, crabs, fricassé of eggs, and pigeons. All this was no dietary flash in the pan. When Mrs Delany dined with friends in Finglas the two courses consisted of 'boyled chicken, bacon, colleyflour epargne, stewed carp, venison pie, chine of mutton and hash', and 'squab pigeons, peas, mushrooms, epargne turkey'. The hospitable hosts had thoughtfully provided a side table laden with 'hot roast beef and cold venison pasty'. The Finglas dessert consisted of eight baskets of fruit.

Mrs Delany's provision for her own guests was on much the same scale. She may, however, have made a little extra effort when entertaining the Primate and the Bishop of Derry (after all her husband was an aspiring dean), because she fed these apparently voracious prelates with 'fish, beefstakes, soup, rabbits and onions, fillet veal, turkey poute, salmon grilde, pickled salmon, quails, little Terrene peas, cream, mushrooms, apple pye, crab, leveret, cheese cakes, blamange, cherries, Dutch cheese, raspberries and cream, almond cream, currants and gooseberries, orange butter.'

She doesn't mention the wines. But then another prelate, Bishop Berkeley, although himself amply doublechinned, ascetically asked in *The Querist* 'whether any kingdom in Europe be so good a customer at Bordeaux as Ireland?'

For what it's worth, let me mention that Mrs Delany can hardly be said to have dug her grave with her teeth. She lived to be eighty-eight.

3

CLUBS AND TAVERNS

1

BARNABY Rich's comment that Dublin's 'whole profit' stood upon ale houses and the selling of ale wasn't a great exaggeration. For most of Dublin's existence as a capital it was much more a socialising centre than a centre of business and industry. Although it was the seat of parliament and of administration, the enactment of Poynings' Law (1494) transferred real governmental power to London because no Irish parliament could be convoked until its programme of legislation had been sanctioned by the English Privy Council and attested by the Great Seal.

In a word, Dublin was politically castrated. It was not just the second city of the Empire but the second city of Ireland, London being the first. The Lord Lieutenant and his court appeared to exercise full regal sway, but the Castle civil servants knew it was all largely a sham. Poynings had clipped his successors' wings and had made it impossible for the English 'garrison' in Ireland to pursue any policy, no matter how desirable for Ireland, which happened to be against English interests.

One effect of the old situation can be felt to this day: that the only real success recognised by the Dubliner is a London success, although in recent years an American success has also begun to count. Hence the brain drain to London and other places, which has outlasted even the notorious brawn drain that weakened and impoverished the country during two centuries. Swift spoke for all Irish authors and painters, sculptors and scholars, actors, musicians and poets when, after a glorious decade of mingling with the mighty on the banks of the Thames, he described his enforced return to his native city to be dean of its most prestigious cathedral as a going into miserable exile.

All Dublin could hope to be was a place where Ireland's well to do enjoyed themselves to the top of their bent, with little need to be concerned with life's whys and wherefores. It wasn't that they were inferior in capacity to English people. The English Mrs Delany found most of her Irish acquaintances 'much the same as in England — a mixture of good and bad; all that I have met with behave themselves very decently, according to their rank, now and then an oddity breaks out, but none so extraordinary but that I can match them in England.'

But because Dubliners had little in their social surroundings to give their life much point beyond the incessant pursuit of pleasure, there grew up the sneering cynical attitude towards serious endeavour for which the city is sadly so well known, an attitude bred by futility and frustration.

The Grand Tour of classical Europe upon which Ireland's and England's *jeunesse dorée* was despatched to broaden its outlook and civilise its tastes, sometimes imbued that *jeunesse* with a determination to come back to Erin and improve the quality of life there. Lord Charlemont, the 'Volunteer Earl', is a textbook example of such idealism proving to be more than a quickly passing phase of youth's energy and enthusiasm.

After his Grand Tour he lingered in London to savour its cultivated pleasures as a member of Samuel Johnson's circle, but then developed a conviction that only by residing in Ireland and setting an enlightened example to his neighbours could the Irish nobleman or landed gentleman usefully serve his country and justify his existence. Charlemont accordingly returned and, although far from being Ireland's richest earl, sought to raise the nation's tastes by building himself Dublin's most refined town house (now the Hugh Lane Art Gallery), and the city's most exquisitely beautiful and useless work of architectural fancy, the Casino at Marino — pure Mozart in stone — and by being the virtual founder of the Royal Irish Academy.

These have proved to be his lasting monuments, although for a long time history considered his true importance to lie in his having been commander-in-chief of the Irish Volunteers, a group formed to help the government to resist an expected French invasion, and armed by the government on that understanding. When the invasion threat slackened the Volunteers took advantage of their arms to extort from England the repeal of Poynings' Act, thus restoring a considerable degree of autonomy to the Irish parliament. The members of what was to

29

be known as 'Grattan's Parliament' promptly used their new powers to earn themselves the reputation of being the most venal and corrupt legislature in Europe. Eighteen years later Grattan's parliamentarians were induced to abolish themselves in an ecstasy of lying, roguery, nefarious bargaining and bribery, to create the Union with England.

All the celebration of Grattan's Parliament (and Grattan), and the Volunteers, makes one wonder whether it's not the law but history is the ass.

2

Charlemont wasn't the only notable builder of his era. There is in many men a passion for building grand houses, a passion resembling the sculptor's to mould and carve, the author's to write books for publishers, the scholar's to garner non-vital knowedge. It's this passion which has given rise to the worldly wise old saying that fools build houses for other men to live in.

The substantial incomes which were squeezed from rack-rented tenants, from wangling personal percentages from various public revenues, and from exploiting the sinecures racket, coupled with the cheapness of labour in Ireland, enabled the Georgians to indulge in wild building sprees. Mansions sprang up all over the country. Dublin became almost another Bath, with its elegant squares and impressive classical public buildings. But pleasure in mansion building obviously ends with the completion of the mansion. The pleasure of living in its grandeur, assuming the builder hasn't run out of life or money or both before the place is finished, is less keen. Charlemont was an exception to the general rule in being able to enjoy living in his own creations, because he was happily occupied in fulfilling the demands of the public position he had made for himself, doing public work which wasn't remunerated and on which he therefore, such are the quirks of human nature, lavished all the more of his time and energy. His vacant hours he could pass contentedly in his fine library and in his art galleries.

Other members of the leisured class, not realising that work is as much a human need as air and food, avoided it, thus making much of their daily life an almost insupportable burden. The business of running their estates was relegated to agents, not always the most efficient. If they attended parliamentary sessions it was either in obedience to the whip or at the prompting of self interest, there being either some measure to be supported because it was to the advantage of their class, or opposed because it wasn't. Or there was some perk or sinecure up for grabs.

Few of them knew of any other way to pass their spare time apart from hunting and whoring, drinking and gambling. Sir Jonah Barrington's descriptions of Irish 'gentlemen' having what they thought was a good time would make any sensible person prefer the lowest circle of hell as an alternative. In Dublin there was no lack of entrepreneurs to provide facilities for the whoring, drinking and gambling. Clubs and taverns abounded, some sited in odd places: for example, the crypt of Christchurch Cathedral.

The degradation of the cathedral began in 1548 with the leasing by its authorities to Arland Ussher, a relation of two Archbishops of Armagh, of part of the crypt which had been turned into a tavern. The practice of sepulchral boozing flourished. By 1633 the Lord Deputy, Thomas Strafford, Earl of Wentworth, complained to Archbishop Laud in London that the entire crypt was now given over to the sale of drink and tobacco:

> where they are pouring either in or
> out their drink offerings and incense
> whilst we above are serving the high God.

He had therefore ordered the removal of the shops, making the Archbishops of Armagh, Dublin and Tuam, or any two of them, responsible for seeing the orders were carried out. He was obliged to issue another ordinance:

> that no person presume to make urine aginst the walls of
> the said church.

It can be mentioned here that pubs and tobacconists weren't the only intrusions into this house of God. Strafford also told Laud that secular buildings had been erected right up against the cathedral walls. He wasn't able to get rid of these, perhaps because they were mostly connected with the law, and indeed housed the law courts themselves. The entrance to the buildings was known as hell. It was a partly arched and gloomy passage some ten feet below the level of the cathedral's present floor, with, over the arch, a horned figure carved in black oak and said to be the devil. The fame of this 'hell' reached Robert Burns —

> But this I am gaun to tell
> Which lately on a night befell,
> is just as true as the deil's in hell
> Or Dublin city.

The Christschurch hell was lined with taverns and snuggeries which, being convenient to the courts, were much patronised by lawyers. Above the taverns were apartments for single men, which were once memorably advertised: 'To be let, furnished apartments in hell. N.B. They are well suited to a lawyer.'

3

As the eighteenth century advanced the taverns and clubs established themselves in more eligible places. The Castle, a noted centre of activity, had lots of officials with plenty of time to discuss affairs over a drink, so many watering holes were opened in the area. Some taverns developed a special character, becoming the recognised meeting places of different professions and the headquarters of political clubs. The lawyers became fond of the Rose Tavern, which stood nearly opposite the present Castle Steps. It remained their rendezvous until the 1770s. 'The Ancient and Most Benevolent Order of the Friendly Brothers of St Patrick' met at the Rose every St Patrick's Day, the prefects at 9.00 a.m. and the 'regulars' at 10.00, after which they attended His Benevolence the President to church. They returned to dine at the Rose at 4.00 p.m.

The Friendly Brothers used pay the debts of selected poor prisoners and their motto, 'Quis Separabit?' was later adopted for the motto of the Knights of St Patrick. They also had the distinction of organising the erection of the first statue put up in what is now O'Connell Street, that of General William Blakeney, the Limerick man who at eighty-four commanded the forces defending Minorca against the French in 1756, his personal exploits including not going to bed for seventy days and nights.

Like many another Dublin future monument, Blakeney's statue of gilt brass, executed by van Nost, was regularly defaced. Finally, six years after being put up, it was knocked off its pedestal, never re-erected, and eventually disappeared.

Another well-known tavern was the Phoenix, in Werburgh Street, very fashionable in its day, used for the quarterly dinners organised by the supporters of the political journalist and agitator Charles Lucas, and a favourite resort of Roscommon men. The Phoenix was also used by the Bar Society for its grand dinners, when guests of honour could be the Speaker of the Irish House of Commons and other dignitaries. In 1752 it was frequented by the Grand Lodge of Freemasons. Castle Street, adjoining Werburgh Street, was lined with taverns, Catlin's being a recognised meeting place for travellers from the North.

The most fashionable of the eighteenth-century clubs was Daly's in College Green, but the most affectionately remembered was the Hellfire. Daly's was opened by one Patrick Daly, a grocer's curate who accumulated enough money to make a start with a premises in Dame Street for drinking and gambling. The profits enabled Daly to hire the fashionable architect Francis Johnston to design a gambling palace for him in College Green, a special path leading to it from the West portico of the Parliament House, since many gentlemen were members of both clubs and could thereby pass the more conveniently from one form of dissipation and extravagance to another. It's said that half the landed property in Ireland regularly changed hands at the gambling tables in Daly's Club.

Daly's Club was originally far more extensive than what's left of the facade today would suggest. It ran from the corner of Angelsey Street to Foster Place and was furnished with grand lustres, inlaid tables, marble chimney pieces and white and gold seats upholstered in silk. The club, which was opened with a banquet on 16 February 1791, continued until 1823, by which time it had come down sadly in the world. The parliament next door had gone out of business in 1800, thus bringing the added disadvantage that the recreational duties of the season were now observed by Ireland's *crème de la crème* in London's West End rather than in College Green.

Dublin's Hellfire Club is often spoken of as if it had an established and continuous association with an ascertainable headquarters, a kind of R.D.S. for the dissolute, with an annual subscription, a set of rules, and candidates blackballed if suspected of underlying respectability. For many years now the stone-roofed hunting lodge on the crest of Montpelier Hill has been confidently identified as the meeting place of the Hellfire Club, much as the organ in St Michan's is pointed out as the very instrument on which Handel composed *Messiah*. The amount of truth in both claims is about the same.

The Hellfire Club seems to have been less an established society than a name adopted by, or bestowed upon, various eighteenth-century groups who aspired to be thought of as the virtuosi of Dublin depravity. The inspiration came from the usual source of Dublin inspirations, London. Three of the London Hellfire Clubs had been suppressed in 1721. These were probably no more than homosexual groups hoping to allay suspicion by assuring enquirers that they were up to nothing worse than celebrating the odd Black Mass. There might have been a similar motivation behind the Dublin formations.

The name Hellfire Club has been associated with the shenanigans of a band of unworthies in Daly's Club in its College Green period, but was more emphatically paraded earlier in the century by a group headed by Richard Parsons, first Earl of Rosse*. In 1735 he and James Worsdale formed a group under the name who used to meet at the Eagle Tavern in Cork Hill (now Lord Edward Street). Worsdale was an immigrant English portrait painter, said to be a natural son of Sir Godfrey Kneller whose pupil he was.

The activities of the Hellfire Club can hardly have been spectacularly evil, seeing that they used the Eagle Tavern, a premises respectable enough to be availed of by the Duke of Hamilton and his duchess (the Roscommon beauty Elizabeth Gunning) when they visited Dublin. Even Worsdale himself was respectable enough to be received in polite society, to join in their amateur theatricals, and to be commissioned by the eminently proper Mrs Conolly of Castletown to do a portrait for her of the Lord Lieutenant, the Duke of Devonshire.

Curiously, Worsdale's portrait group of Hellfire Club members (now in the National Gallery of Ireland) doesn't include Lord Rosse. The five figures, represented quite unsensationally as seated or standing around a table, are Lord Santry, Colonel Clements, Colonel Ponsonby, Colonel St George and Mr Luttrell. The only one of them to do a good PR job on behalf of the Hellfire Club was Lord Santry. In 1739, shortly after the

*Of the first creation, which died out in 1764. The title was revived in 1806 and the line has continued in unimpeachable respectability to the present day.

34

picture is deemed to have been painted, he was brought before the Irish House of Lords to be tried for the murder of a footman, Loughlin Murphy. He was found guilty, sentenced to hang, and his estates were forfeited to the Crown. But through the mediation of the Lord Lieutenant, the Duke of Devonshire, and several other Irish peers, George II was induced to pardon Lord Santry and to restore his estates two years later.

Lord Rosse died in 1741 in his early forties. An amusing story is told of how, with one foot in the grave, he could still kick the other heel in the air. The vicar of St Anne's in Dawson Street, casting his dying parishioner in the role of Don Giovanni and himself as the Commendatore, sent him a letter urging him to repent of his sins (with list enclosed) before it was too late. Rosse, noticing that the letter had no superscription and began with a simple 'My lord', re-sealed it and addressed it to the local pillar of society, the frail, puny, fastidious little Earl of Kildare who was said to keep his gloves on even while caressing his wife.

Lord Kildare, outraged at being accused of grievous sins (the least of which was fornication), hurried to the archbishop to complain about the lunatic vicar. It took some time to straighten out this piece of *commedia dell' arte,* Lord Rosse not surviving to enjoy fully his splendid joke. He departed this life only a few hours after perpetrating it. Still chuckling, one hopes.

4

Dublin's ordinary citizens indulged their high spirits in the traditional ways: wine, women and song. But they also observed certain official festivities, dating from medieval times, which were rather like the St Patrick's Day parades of today.

Before the Municipal Reform Act of the 1840s abolished the city's trade guilds, the traders were grouped into twenty-five bodies, each with its patron saint or classical hero, whose image was dressed in the garments appropriate to the trade for festive occasions. The images were carried in the mayoral procession, the masters on horseback, the journeymen on foot, the apprentices in the rear. Most of the guilds also had large wagons, drawn by eight or ten carthorses, on which were built high platforms festooned with ribbons and draperies. Workers plied their trade on the platform as if in their shop, throwing samples of their products to the crowd below.

The blacksmiths, deemed the most picturesque of all, not only had a forge and fire on their wagon, but enlivened the show with romantic interest. Their wagon was followed by a phaeton with a beautiful girl dressed as the wife of their patron Vulcan. With her were half a dozen children attired as Cupids, aiming their arrows at the women bystanders. Vulcan in coal black armour and Mars in silver armour with feathers and coloured horsehair, rode on either side of the phaeton, Madame Vulcan playing for laughs by openly flirting with Mars.

The tailors quite frankly went for laughs. They would ride crosslegged on spirited horses, so that they spent more time sprawling in the dust than in the saddle. But it would have been the guild of merchants (brokers and financiers) who would have most amused the cynics. The money men, unable to find a patron saint or a classical hero, presented a ship on wheels manned by sailors. Their emblem was an outsize shamrock.

There was a great increase in the number of clubs for all classes during the nineteenth and early twentieth centuries. The workingmen's clubs were mostly of the self-improving kind, combining education, spiritual uplift and the promotion of tea and coffee as substitutes for alcohol. There were clubs for amateur artists, rowing enthusiasts, riflemen, chess players, lawyers, yachtsmen, and refuges from women like the Dublin University Club, the St Stephen's Green, the Sackville and the Kildare Street, which, unlike Daly's and the Hellfire, were too dull to have histories.

4

BEGGARS AND FOUNDLINGS

1

THE 'poor mouth' has long been a noted Irish characteristic, and in Dublin begging became an art form. Some beggars were celebrities, like Billy-in-the-Bowl who flourished in the 1780s and pursued his vocation in the Stoneybatter-Grangegorman area.

Billy was literally in a bowl made of iron and fitted with wheels, for he had been born without legs. But nature, with a touch of remorse, gave him soulfully luminous dark eyes, a fine nose and mouth, and a mop of rich brown curly hair. His combination of misfortune and charm made him a special pet with the women of Stoneybatter and Grangegorman. When he appeared the servant girls would raise the cry 'It's Billy-in-the-Bowl, ma'am,' and housewives were said to authorise the packing of his bowl with beef, bread and dainties.

But Billy supplemented these alms with a sinister sideline. He used to spend some evenings hidden behind a hedge on a lonely path beyond the city, emerging to beg from the solitary traveller. If the traveller ventured within reach, Billy seized him — he had phenomenally strong arms — killed him and robbed him. The killing would have been necessary because Billy was so easily identifiable, and since Billy would have struck only when there were no witnesses he remained unsuspected.

But one evening he pushed his luck too far. Two well-to-do ladies with gold watches, bracelets and diamond rings were strolling along what was then known as Richardson's Lane (now part of Collins' Barracks). Billy appeared with his customary plea and managed to seize both women. But one managed to wind her hand in his hair and press her thumb into his eye. Billy had to let go and the women fled back to their friends in Manor Street. A posse was sent after him and he was caught hiding

37

behind a hedge. His was a capital offence, but he was let off with life imprisonment and spent the remainder of his days in Newgate in Green Street, performing such hard labour as his disability allowed.

While there was always some sympathy for the handicapped or disabled, there was little for obviously ablebodied beggars. These caused much irritation and resentment amongst the citizens. Even the fundamentally goodnatured Dean Swift was exasperated by beggars who refused to stay in their own parish but very sensibly moved around the city in search of the sweetest honey of benevolence.

In 1737 Swift published *A Proposal for giving Badges to the Beggars in all the parishes of Dublin*, reviving the same proposal he had made eleven years earlier to the Archbishop of Dublin. He recommended the issue of metal badges to be worn by the poor of the various parishes, identifying their parish, and so preventing them from begging outside it. The archbishop had instructed his clergy to adopt the proposal but this had little effect:

> by the fraud, perverseness or pride of the said poor, several of them openly protesting 'they will never submit to wear the said badges'. And of those who received them, almost everyone keep them in their pockets, or hang them in a string about their necks, or fasten them under their coats, not to be seen, by which means the whole design is eluded.

By modern notions the beggars would be thought right to have refused to be tagged like animals, and that other Dubliner Oscar Wilde's dictum that it is finer to steal than to beg has many sympathisers. Yet Swift remains oddly old fashioned but quite up to date in his angry denunciation of the unbadged beggars:

> They are too lazy to work, they are not afraid to steal, nor ashamed to beg; and yet are too proud to be seen with a badge, as many of them have confessed to me, and not a few in very injurious terms, particularly the females. They all look upon such an obligation as a high indignity done to their office.

He went on to declare that he had stopped giving even a farthing to a street beggar and was urging fellow pedestrians to follow his example. ('However, as to persons in coaches and chairs, they bear but little of the persecution we suffer, and are willing to leave it entirely upon us.') He added rather pharisaically that nineteen in twenty of those who were reduced to starvation did not become so by act of God but from their own idleness, attended with all manner of vices, particularly drunkenness, thievery, and cheating.

> To say the truth, there is not a more undeserving vicious race of human kind than the bulk of those who are reduced to beggary, even in this beggarly country. . . . As this is the only Christian country where people contrary to the old maxim, are the poverty and not the riches of the nation, so, the blessing of increase and multiply is by us converted into a curse; and, as marriage hath been ever countenanced in all free countries, so we should be less miserable if it were discouraged in ours, as far as can be consistent with Christianity.

But neither badging nor any other scheme could reduce the begging, which remained as a plague for the ordinary citizen who couldn't stir out of doors without being beset by clutching hands and whining voices. Clergymen were especially vulnerable, as the beggars knew well. Archbishop Whately once tried a lofty put-down, telling a beggarwoman outside his palace in St Stephen's Green that he never gave to anyone begging in the street.

'Then', she replied, 'where would your Grace desire me to wait upon you?'

2

Begging by letter flourished in Dublin in the middle of the nineteenth century, a gang in Bridgefoot Street operating the racket on efficient business lines. From their head office poured piteous appeals from distressed widows, disconsolate orphans, Waterloo veterans, and businessmen who had fallen on hard times through no fault of their own. There was the inevitable clergyman's widow with four female children (eldest only eleven) whose 'pious, exemplary and most affectionate partner had died of malignant fever contracted while whispering words of Christian consolation to the departing sinner, and imparting the joyful assurance that the life flickering away would be re-kindled in a lamp of everlasting duration and unvarying brilliance.'

Although the widow was resigned to her fate she felt she was 'not forbidden to hope that the blessed spirit of charity would be manifested in her relief, and in shielding her helpless, artless babes from the privations of distress in their infancy; and from the still more fearful danger of being, in advanced youth, exposed to the snares of sin and its depraving consequences.' Subsequent investigation by the police revealed that the 'widow' succeeded in getting £5 from no less a person than the Lord Chief Justice himself for this effusion.

A 'military lady', widow of a colour sergeant who had been wounded in India and then drowned while being invalided home, reached her native Dublin with her eight orphans only to discover that 'all her relations had died or emigrated', leaving her 'friendless and alone'. This netted £3 from Lady Blakeney.

The most original plea came from a 'commercial traveller' who for several years had 'supported a numerous and interesting family by his industry and intelligence'. Unfortunately, while in Co. Tipperary during a contested election he incautiously 'expressed a wish for the success of the Conservative candidate'. He was promptly set upon by the opposition and 'beaten so as to produce paralysis of his lower extremities'. Nothing remained for him but 'to entreat the humane consideration of one who could not, if the public testimony to her generous disposition was to be credited, refuse to sympathise with a parent whose help-lessness compelled him to witness with unavailing anguish, the poignant miseries of the offspring he had hoped by his honest exertions to have supported, without the necessity of soliciting that aid which nothing but the most absolute destitution could reconcile him to implore.'

We are not told how much, if anything, this minor master-piece elicited.

The police swooped on the Bridgefoot Street gang, arresting forty-one of them and discovering that they had counterfeit seals of the cities of Cork, Waterford, Limerick, Sligo, Drogheda, Dublin, Liverpool, Bristol, Hamburg, Le Havre and New York. These were used in forged certificates and attestations. But the arrests failed to stamp out the racket. It broke out again and again and no doubt will continue to the end of time.

A possibly more acceptable kind of professional beggar was the clergyman who preached charity sermons, a form of eccles-iastical entertainment much enjoyed by the Victorians. Rev.

Walter Blake Kirwan (1754-1805) was a legendary performer. Born in Galway to Catholic parents, he was sent to St Omer to study for the priesthood. After seven or eight years as a priest he became a Protestant minister and in 1787 was appointed assistant curate at St Peter's in Aungier Street, 'the parish church of Dublin', and highly fashionable. (It was demolished in 1983.) He was soon acknowledged to be the city's top clerical tear jerker. As an oratorical marksman he was superb. He scored bullseye after bullseye on his hearers' emotions, in spite of his unprepossessing appearance. Sir Jonah Barrington tells us that 'There was an air of discontent in his looks, and a sharpness in his features which, in the aggregate, amounted to something not distant from repulsion.'

But the takings at the St Peter's annual charity sermon jumped from £200 to £1,000 when Kirwan performed. Pointing to the graveyard outside he would say: 'If they who lie there, whose place you now occupy, and whose riches you possess (God only knows how you possess!) — if they, I say, were at this moment to appear amongst you — don't tremble! — it would not be to reclaim their wealth but to bear testimony to its vanity.'

The plate would then be taken around by a titled lady.

Kirwan's masterpiece was his three-word sermon on behalf of the Dublin orphans, a group of whom were stationed in the aisle for the occasion. Climbing into the pulpit as if on his last legs, he gazed mournfully at the orphans for what seemed an age. Then he sobbed out his three words: 'There they are.' With his hands over his face he stumbled from the pulpit and made a tearful exit, while the church echoed with sobs, groans and the chink of coin and jewel on the collection plates. The takings were £1,122, over £60,000 in modern values.

The sequel was interesting. The following day most of the congregation returned sheepishly to the vestry to ask if they could have their watches and jewels back in return for a token cash payment.

Kirwan was in 1800 appointed Dean of Killala, where the stipend reflected the size of the cathedral: £150 a year. He remained an absentee, living in Mount Pleasant, Ranelagh, where he died in October 1805, aged fifty-one. His widow was given a state pension of £300 a year.

Curiously, the Catholic champion Dublin preacher was another Galwayman, Fr. Tom Burke, O.P.

41

3

Dublin's orphans and foundlings were in theory well cared for in the city's Foundling Hospital, an institution officially in charge of the Corporation. The board of governors included the Archbishops of Armagh and of Dublin, with others of the great and good, which didn't prevent the mortality rate and the general administration of the place being an obscene scandal even by Corporation standards. At last even a Chief Secretary, Sir John Blaquiere, was moved to protest, but the Corporation was able, as usual, to muster defenders. Henry Grattan, keeping a patriotic eye to the safety of his parliamentary seat as a Member for Dublin city, put on the mantle of Dr Pangloss and assured his fellow citizens that all was for the best in the best of all possible foundling hospitals. (He also opposed the Dublin Police Bill for its proposal to saddle the ratepayers with the cost of maintaining a constabulary in the most saintly of all possible cities.)

Grattan might appear to have been outdone in humbug by the Foundling Hospital chaplain who, mentioning that he had noticed a foundling being lashed twelve times with the cat, added that he had never seen a child 'cruelly treated' there. Other witnesses mentioned the cases of the boy who complained about the bad bread (twenty lashes and the stocks), and of the seven or eight year old who was given a mere eight or nine lashes for not getting quickly enough into bed. No cruelty was perceived even in the sixty lashes awarded to a boy whose leg had an iron weight affixed to it as well. But before we righteously condemn such people for repulsive hypocrisy, let us remember that this was an age which approved of sentences of five hundred and a thousand lashes for erring soldiers. By such standards sixty lashes were no more than a salutary admonishment which would do a child all the good in the world. But no such excuses can be found for the institution's other crimes against the young.

The Foundling Hospital, which existed from 1703 until 1832, was established chiefly to deal with the child beggar problem. At first no infants were to be received, the age limits for admission being five to sixteen. Any child surviving to sixteen was apprenticed to some Protestant tradesman.

Since the Foundling Hospital was governed and staffed only by Protestants, it was held in hatred and contempt by the Catholics. The children were often attacked while being paraded through the streets to be inspected by the Lord Mayor and other dignitaries. By the 1750s the number of admissions had trebled, and when the lower age limit was done away with so that infants could be taken in the admissions soon reached a tenfold increase. This was largely owing to children being brought to the hospital from all parts of the country.

Admission was facilitated by the old device of a 'turning wheel', with no questions asked. A basket was affixed to a wheel built into the hospital gate. The children were placed in the basket and a bell rung, the wheel being then turned inwards by the porter on duty.

The mortality rate for Foundling babies was reckoned to be at least 80 per cent, a principal cause of death being murder. For when the governors set up a scheme whereby infants were to be fostered by outside nurses who were paid £2 a year for each infant, the women took the children and the small advance payment and then killed them. In 1737 the bodies of thirteen branded infants were discovered in a sandpit, one of the findings of Sir John Blaquiere's parliamentary committee of inquiry being that the officers of the hospital sought the destruction of the foundlings by giving them to 'profligate barbarous nurses'. All through the eighteenth century the most damning reports came to light of what was happening in the hospital. For instance, between 1791 and 1796 some ten thousand children were admitted. Of these, 5,216 were treated in the 'infirmary'. Only *one* recovered. In the first quarter of 1795, out of 540 admitted 440 died.

To be sent to the infirmary was virtually to be sentenced to death. So as not to waste 'good' clothes on the infants they were stripped à la Belsen, dressed in rags, placed five or six in a cradle 'swarming with vermin' and covered with blankets which had already been officially discarded as unusable.

Then there was the legendary 'Bottle', believed to be compounded from diacodium, a syrup of poppies. The hospital nurse in evidence under oath said that the children were dosed indiscriminately with 'The Bottle'. She claimed to have understood that it was a 'composing draught' because 'the children were easy for an hour or two after taking it'. In the end it killed them off. Stories were told of babies lying dead in their cot for days, apparently without anyone noticing. Eventually the little corpses were dropped into a big coffin kept under the stairs. Only when a full load was obtained was the coffin buried. The graveyard was the hospital yard itself, which was so over-packed with the dead that the digging of a new grave brought other remains to the surface.

Parliamentary committees were set up again and again to investigate the Foundling Hospital, and the Corporation was denounced as the body ultimately responsible for the state of affairs there. But recommendations were ignored.

You may wonder why concerned individuals did not intervene. There were several reasons. It was virtually impossible for a private citizen to intervene effectively in the affairs of a public institution governed by a body of men who included *ex officio* the Archbishop of Dublin. Criticism and protest were about all that could be done, and these are notoriously of little use unless supported by a vigorous and continuing campaign which wins ever increasing public support. There was however one highly successful intervention by an individual in the hospital's affairs. It was by a Kerrywoman, Lady Arbella (her own spelling) Denny, and she would hardly have been able to get her foot across the Foundling door, in spite of her determined character, had she not been the daughter of the first Earl of Kerry and aunt of the British prime minister Lord Shelburne.

4

Arbella Fitzmaurice (1707-1792) married a man much her senior, and on being widowed in her thirties declared that never again would she go into servitude by taking a husband.* She occupied herself by organising a committee of fashionable ladies (the only kind available) to help clear up the administrative mess at the hospital. The task was too much like hard work for the fashionable ladies. They melted away, leaving Arbella to get along on her own. Which she did. (She may have been very relieved to be rid of her committee.)

It was she who hired new nurses and awarded bonuses to those who worked well. She spent over £4,000, raised from friends and from her own money, on enlarging and improving the hospital buildings and introduced a special clock which struck every 20

---

*Arbella evidently had a good opinion of herself. When she visited Ballymote, Co. Sligo, where her family (the Fitzmaurices) owned property, she caused an obelisk to be erected in her own honour on a nearby hill. The obelisk survived until 1960s, when some too-near digging caused it to tumble down.

minutes when 'all ye infants that are not asleep must be discreetly fed'. A relation designed 'a most useful bottle resembling a human breast', which moved the Foundling governors to present the inventress with a gold box.

Best of all, perhaps, Arbella was able to put the fear of God into those sadists and flagellomaniacs who swarm to jobs involving the control of children. Had she been succeeded at the hospital by another such capable woman all would have been well. But on reaching her seventies she had to retire without having trained a successor. Perhaps she assumed that her reforms would be permanent. When she died in 1792 aged eighty-five, the old state of affairs returned, until finally, in 1832, the Foundling Hospital was abolished unlamented.

5

PHILANTHROPISTS

1

D UBLIN appears to have had more than the normal quota
of philanthropists for a city of its size and population. Apart
from those medieval businessmen and entrepreneurs who, as
death approached, nervously remembered in their wills to leave
sums to provide almshouses for respectable widows or spinsters,
or weekly loaves of bread for the poor of the parish, there were men
and women who, like Arbella Denny, exercised their talent for
improving the world during their lifetime. And Dublin provided
plenty of scope for such talents.

The rapid increase in poverty, distress and disease early in the
century generated a feeling of social concern. Swift is said to
have applied his principle of living on one-third of his income,
saving a third, and giving away a third. So far as his means
allowed, he operated a kind of one-man social welfare state in
the Liberties, partly by personally distributing alms, partly by
making loans at low interest to tradesmen who needed a little
capital to develop their business. Sometimes his feelings over-
came him. One such occasion impelled him to write his
notorious *Modest Proposal for Preventing the Children of Poor People
from being a Burthern to Their Parents or Country.*

> I have been assured by a very knowing American of my
> acquaintance in London, that a young healthy child well
> nursed is at a year old a most delicious, nourishing, and
> wholesome food, whether stewed, roasted, baked, or
> boiled, and I make no doubt that it will equally serve in a
> fricassee, or a ragout.

This emotional explosion may have been a case of literary over-
kill, causing more readers to turn away in genteel revulsion than
move them to some practical gesture. Swift had of course let it be

known that his own great practical gesture would be made in due time.

> He gave the little wealth he had
>   To build a house for fools and mad;
> And show'd, by one satiric touch,
>   No nation wanted it so much.

Meanwhile, since the parliamentarians and the city fathers were too busy feathering their own nests to have much energy left for doing their public duty, the task of providing hospitals, once the care of the great religious orders, was left to private individuals.

In the late 1720s a Charitable Infirmary, later to flower as Jervis Street Hospital, was opened in a small house in Cook Street. Mercer's and Steevens's Hospitals were opened soon afterwards. Mercer's was founded by Mrs Mary Mercer, who made over for the purpose a large stone building she owned in Stephen Street. (The building was on the site of the ancient leper hospital of St Stephen.) Mercer's opened in 1734, closing two hundred and fifty years later as part of a governmental rationalisation scheme whereby, if you drop or are dropped in the inner city, there is no inner city hospital to treat you, and you are expected to survive until the ambulance succeeds in getting you to one of the mammoth institutions in the suburbs.

A year before Mercer's, following twelve years of fund collecting and building, Steevens's opened its door.

Grizel Steevens was the daughter of a Cromwellian immigrant. Her brother, a doctor, Professor of Physic at Trinity College and twice elected president of the College of Physicians, left his fortune in trust for Grizel. After her death it was to go towards founding a public hospital. But three years after coming into her inheritance, Grizel decided to go ahead with the hospital herself. She wasn't far off sixty, was unmarried, and no doubt was attracted by the prospect of bringing a major purpose into her life with, in due course, the added reward of being boss of an important institution.

She therefore appointed her own committee. Included were the archbishop, a senior judge, and one of the kind of businessmen known in Dublin by the magniloquent title of merchant prince. As is usual when women form such committees, Grizel declined to have any other woman on it, so that it was for herself

47

alone that fourteen stately male bottoms heaved themselves off their chairs whenever Grizel, now preferring to be called Madame Steevens, entered the room for a meeting.

Grizel was no beauty, her portrait, which still hangs in the hospital boardroom, showing that she had rather masculine features. Her practice of wearing a veil when out of doors gave rise to the preposterous rumour that she had a pig's snout for a nose. The rumour remained current even after she countered it by sitting unveiled beside an open window so that passers-by could see for themselves that she was not disfigured. Indeed the rumour was presently embellished with a historical basis. The snout, it was said, was the result of a beggarwoman's curse. The beggarwoman, with a child at her breast and a tribe of them at her heels, had implored Grizel's mother for alms and had been repulsed with 'Get away! You're like an old sow with a litter of bonhams.' The beggar retorted with a wish that the other woman's next child might be like a pig — and the next child was Grizel.

Steevens's Hospital is charmingly built around a courtyard framed with arches to form a kind of piazza. The architect, Colonel Thomas Burgh, was a member of the hospital committee and had designed Trinity College Library, the original custom house, St Werburgh's and the Royal (Collins) Barracks. Grizel had chosen well. She had reserved £150 of her inheritance to herself for life, and stipulated that she was to be allowed live in the hospital. Rooms on the left of the entrance gate are pointed out as hers.

Edward Worth, a physician at the hospital, and one of the governors, bequeated his medical library of four thousand volumes to Steevens' for the use of the doctors. These gentlemen don't appear to have availed themselves much of this facility, for even after more than two and a half centuries most of the volumes are in mint condition. It is pleasant to be able to add that the successive honorary keepers of the Worth Library have treated it with loving care.

Next door to Steevens's is St Patrick's Hospital, to the foundation of which Swift had bequeathed the bulk of his fortune, and the governors of Steevens's a site. The architect was George Semple who, incidentally, designed the spire which, after Swift's death, was added to the ancient tower of his cathedral.

But the prince of Dublin's hospital founders was Bartholomew

48

Mosse, whose maternity hospital has become internationally famous in its own right as The Rotunda.

2

Those born in the Rotunda are apt to assume that the hospital is in fact the Rotunda (or Rotundo as it used to be called). But the name properly belongs to the entertainment room later put up to provide a source of income, the institution itself being officially the Lying-In Hospital. It was not only the first of its kind in these islands but the most palatial. Complaints were made while it was being built that it looked more like a nobleman's mansion that a refuge for the pregnant needy.

Bartholomew Mosse was born around 1712 in Portlaoise, a town he would have known as Maryborough. He was the son of the rector and began his career as an army surgeon, serving abroad. But on his return to Ireland he switched to midwifery and, moved by the miserable conditions in which the poorer Dublin women gave birth — sometimes actually on the roadside — resolved to improve their lot. With the help of friends he acquired a premises in what is now South Great George's Street, and opened it as a maternity hospital. Although the house was centrally situated and commodious (three storeys) he probably got it cheap since it had previously been occupied by Madame Violante, who trained little girls to dance upon the tight rope (one of them the future stage star Peg Woffington), and is suspected of providing other services for gentlemen.

In this little hospital's first year more than two hundred babies were born. Nearly half died, not through negligence as at the Foundling Hospital, but because infant mortality was very high in those days in all social classes.

Mosse financed the South Great George's Street hospital much as he would later finance the Lying-In Hospital, by lotteries and concerts. He diverted £500 of the proceeds into purchasing the lease of the four acres of ground on which the Rotunda complex now stands. He walled in the ground, landscaped it, put up a concert hall and a coffee room and charged the public a shilling a head for admission to an elegant musical entertainment.

This venture proved profitable. Mosse was able to get the most fashionable architect of the day, Richard Castle, to design

49

a handsome hospital. The foundation stone was laid by the lord mayor in 1751, but Castle had died the previous year and it was John Ensor who supervised the construction work. The hospital was opened by the lord lieutenant, the Duke of Bedford, on 8 December 1757, a thing which was no hindrance to Mosse when he came to putting the squeeze on parliament and the Corporation for grants in aid.

Mosse's success owed much to his 'thinking big'. The hospital was on the grand scale, being one of the city's architectural sights (although later critics were less than ecstatic about the facade and the too slender tower and cupola). But Mosse excelled himself in the embellishment of the chapel, a thing which would have impressed his father the rector and his own second wife, the daughter of an archdeacon. He brought in from the continent one Barthelemy Cramillion to design and execute the ceiling plasterwork for a fee of five hundred guineas. The result is an outburst, unique in Ireland, of baroque exuberance: the stuccodore's reply to Handel's Music for the Royal Fireworks. Mosse's pleasure grounds and buildings, flatteringly likened to those of London, continued for many years to help the hospital funds. Other assembly rooms were built after his death. These have continued to render good service to the city down to this day, one of them as the Gate Theatre. The hospital itself continues to be internationally famous for its excellence.

Bartholomew Mosse's reign as first Master of the Lying-In Hospital lasted only two years, for he contracted some obscure disease and died in 1759, aged forty-seven. He was buried in the old cemetery at Donnybrook, a place whose peculiarity is that only the graves of nonentities are clearly identifiable. There's absolutely no clue as to the last resting places of the notables.

3

Three other notables in the philanthropic line were immigrants from Carlow. These were James Haughton and his son Samuel, and Thomas Pleasants.

Pleasants (1728-1818) has his admirers, but although his long and wordy will has amused many a reader in its time, its provisions reveal that his name somewhat belied his nature. Little is known about his early life. He is believed to have been trained for the Bar but was never called, passing his youth and middle age obscurely until in his sixtieth year he married Mildred, second of the three daughters of a rich Dublin surgeon, George Daunt of South William Street. The surgeon, still remembered in medical history as the inventor of improved instruments for performing lithotomy, had bequeathed £30,000 apiece to his daughters, and the girls agreed to make wills in each other's favour.

Mildred survived her sisters, ending up with the entire legacy which, after a certain amount of chopping and changing in her testamentary intentions towards Pleasants, according to her mood, she finally left to him. He outlived her for four years and, having done his own share of ill-tempered tinkering with the minor bequests to his domestic servants, made it clear that sooner than let his wife's family, 'the accursed Daunts', get their hands on a penny of the money, he would leave for charitable purposes what he hadn't already spent on good works.

Almost immediately after coming into the money he financed the building of the Stove Tenter House in Cork Street in which the local weavers could dry and stretch their fabrics in bad weather. That same year he donated £4,000 to the Meath Hospital for a new operating theatre, with another £2,000 to buy wine and nourishing food for needy patients. Various other hospitals benefited by his will: the Fever Hospital was left £5,000, the Hospital for Incurables the same, St Bridget's Parish School and the Meath Charitable Loan £3,000 apiece, and so on. The bequests, by the way, were to be paid in his Grand Canal Debentures, which at the time stood at about 25 per cent below par.

His chief benefaction however was the school for orphaned Protestant girls. This was to be established after his death at his home, 67 Lower Camden Street, no alterations to which were to be made except the most necessary for its new purpose. His bedroom and sittingroom, with their furniture, were to be allocated to the matron, but she had no exclusive rights in the back garden. This was to be maintained as it was for the girls' recreation, and no vegetables were to be grown there because they could be had cheaper at the market. The girls were to be maintained until of marriageable age, when they were to be dowried according to merit and married off to genuine Protestants. The Pleasants Asylum for Female Orphans, as it was called, got off to a good start. A visitor in April 1819 reported that 'I found on the strictest examination every kind of food of the best quality — the dinner prepared was prime beef nicely served, fit for children in the first rank of life.' In later times the girls were no longer compulsorily matched to anyone but were educated at Alexandra School and then assisted to train for suitable professions. In the 1950s the Asylum departed from Camden Street on amalgamating with the Kirwan House Institution in Sandford Road.

The original Pleasants' will was destroyed in the Four Courts holocaust in 1922, but copies survive. One is a showpiece at the Public Records Office. To be fair to Pleasants, in cutting his in-laws out of his will he was no more than carrying out his wife's intentions, for long before Mildred died she had made it clear that they needn't hope to be left a penny. Having nothing to lose they wasted no civility on Mildred or upon her newly married husband, whom they must have looked upon as a fortune hunter. Thus when Mildred died the widower, then in his eighty-sixth year, was unceremoniously bundled out of the Daunt house in South William Street: yet another reason for revenging himself when will-making time came around.

The will contains many snide remarks about the Daunts, and 'beloved Milly' is quoted with relish as saying that 'she knew none of her family that was worthy of her attention'. In one of the autobiographical digressions in the will Pleasants records that at one time Milly intended to leave him only £400 a year because, as he explains, she feared that his extremely charitable disposition would make him the prey of swindlers. In another will she left him only £200, which was to punish him for objecting to her being bossed by her eldest sister when they were living in South William Street. His own will tinkerings included putting his maidservants Mary and Eliza down for £500 apiece, then they were out without a penny, then they were put back, then knocked out, and so on. They were also tormented with threats of unequal legacies. For example, Eliza was to get £10 more than Mary partly to compensate her for ill-usage at Mary's hands, partly on account of her 'wonderful exertions' the night the rain poured into Pleasants' bedroom because of the roguery of a slater 'who tore up the roof to make a job for himself'.

The coachman got £200 for being sober and punctual 'and an excellent son to his mother, spending all his spare time with her'.

The cook was left the copper utensils she kept so bright, the apothecary's assistant was rewarded with £5 for being obliging and attentive. Pleasants' collection of busts and paintings (including portraits by Reynolds and Hogarth) would have gone to a female relation had she married and settled in Dublin, 'but England seems to have got possession of her and a shilling's worth of them to go there I would never assent to'. So these pictures, and the more valuable of his books, went to the Royal Dublin Society instead.

In writing about Milly he becomes touchingly poetical. He was to be buried in her grave in St Bride's churchyard, her slippers to be

> laid crossways on my breast, next to my heart, for I have, since her most sincerely lamented death, constantly had them under my pillow, kissed them and press'd them to my heart every night, going to bed, and the same in the morning rising. I request that her coffin may not be disburb'd, but mine let down gently, on it. And I hope our dust may mix as our loves blended. I married her for love: I lived with her for love, and I shall die, in the enthusiastic belief that we will be permitted to know each other, in the next life; and in celestial union, enjoy to all eternity celestial bliss.

Unfortunately Thomas Pleasants and Mildred weren't allowed an undisturbed eternity, for in 1898 St Bride's church was demolished and the contents of its graveyard removed to a suburban cemetery.

4

Thomas Pleasants and the Haughtons provide ammunition for those who find something unlikable about philanthropists. The Haughton family, Carlovians like Pleasants, established a residence in Dublin for convenience in carrying on their corn business. James Haughton and his son Samuel were humanitarians, the father an active campaigner against hanging, the son a scientific searcher out of ways to make hanging more efficient and therefore less painful. Both of them, as is the case with many humanitarians, hardly looked the part. Samuel (1821-18797), although in holy orders as well as being a medical doctor and a professor of geology in Trinity College, was much more jovial and sociable than his portrait suggests. His father (1795-1873) in appearance strongly suggested Ivan the Terrible with a hangover, a double injustice because apart from his natural kindness he was an apostle of temperance who laboured hard with Father Mathew and the Carmelite Father John Spratt of Whitefriars Street Priory at the uphill task of making Ireland dry. James was a great campaigner for Sunday opening, not of pubs but of public amusements and amenities. He argued that if the working man had something interesting to do on his day off (and in those times that meant just Sunday), then he wouldn't spend the whole day in the pubs to the ruin of his health and his family. James believed that a good way to keep the working class amused on Sundays would be to open the Botanic Gardens and the Zoo, although this idea was open to the criticism that the average family's pleasure and interest in visiting these places would hardly survive weekly repetition. An adequate reply to this would be that a start has to be made somewhere. However it wasn't on the ground of possible boredom that the Royal Dublin Society, which then had charge of the Botanic Gardens, opposed Haughton's proposal. They maintained that if the working man and his family were let into the Gardens they would leave the place a dust heap after them. Common sense and decency prevailed however, and the Gardens were given a Sunday opening. In due course the Zoo too was opened on Sundays at an admission of one penny, and, again thanks chiefly to James Haughton, the People's Garden was established in the Phoenix Park.

Unfortunately James Haughton's relations with Father Mathew weren't of the smoothest. When the Apostle of Temperance got his finances into a tangle, James organised a committee to untangle them. The committee, which included the Duke of Leinster, declined to hand over any of the funds collected until Father Mathew had given them all the documents relating to his money matters. Father Mathew declined the offer on these terms, reporting to his friend Gavan Duffy that this 'self-elected' group wanted him

> to unfold to them my most private affairs, allow them to arrange with creditors, and receive from them whatever pittance they deem sufficient to supply my daily wants. To

54

this I will never submit. I would rather take a staff in my hand and *walk* to the temperance meetings, and depend for support on the affection of my poor teetotallers.

No committee, even with a duke aboard, was likely to intimidate Father Mathew, for in addition to his normal Irish priestly inhumility he was closely related to the Earl of Llandaff, master of many rich Tipperary acres, and accordingly felt able to stand up to any other blueblood.

But although the seeds of James Haughton's philanthropy might now and then fall on stony ground, they usually found fertile soil. In 1837, for instance, he helped to found the Dublin Mechanics' Institute. Its objective was 'the scientific and literary improvement of the operative classes . . . by means of a Reading Room, well supplied with all the literary and scientific periodicals of the day; a Lending Library, consisting of many hundred well selected volumes; courses of lectures, delivered periodically, to which the members are admitted gratuitously, with the privilege of introducing a lady'. The annual subscription was ten shillings, membership did not require nomination or election and was open to women, who had the power to bring a friend to lectures. Membership benefits included, besides books and lectures, admission to the Northumberland Baths at reduced rates, likewise to Monsieur Maccaud's Gymnasium in Grafton Street (four shillings per quarter); and Mr Nelson, Artist, Grafton Street, offered to take 'Daguerrotype portraits' of members at seven shillings and sixpence each. The institute later moved to Lower Abbey Street to a small building which with typical Dublin magniloquence had been named the Royal Irish Opera House. But the Mechanics' Institute drew less and less support as the years passed. The lecture room-cum-concert hall of which high hopes had been held in the early days was reduced to staging cheap variety turns, the upper storeys were given over to tenements, and by the turn of the century the Institute was a dead duck. The premises later became part of the Abbey Theatre.

James's son Samuel Haughton was famous in his day as a mathematician, physicist, zoologist but most of all for providing a scientific basis for long-drop hanging. The authorities had long been aware that a long drop made for a more merciful death. But a long drop could also wrench the head off the victim, so executioners preferred a short drop which strangled him relatively slowly. Haughton drew up a table of drop lengths related to the weight of the victim, calculated to ensure speedy death without unacceptable mutilation. He is said to have erected a gallows in his laboratory, using for experiments the corpses allocated to him as a doctor.

His recommendations were officially adopted in Ireland, but the first execution resulted in a decapitation, Haughton had prescribed a silken rope and forgot to allow for its elasticity. Having ordered a return to traditional hemp he announced that he would attend the next execution as an observer. He stationed himself in the pit below the trapdoor, this time forgetting the length of his own long drop and was nearly brained by the victim's heels. But when describing the incident years later to the composer Villiers Stanford, he boasted 'But there wasn't as much as a kick in him'.

5

Pleasants and the Haughtons had several rivals in the philanthropy game. To take an example almost at random: four merchants came together in 1875 to found the City of Dublin Workingmen's Club which, being situated first in Fishamble Street and later at 10 Wellington Quay, seemed to be the southside's answer to the Mechanics' Institute on the other bank of the Liffey. The founders were prominent Dubliners: there was the optician Isaac Yeates; the wholesale grocer Jonathan Hogg; John Lemass, draper and grandfather of the illustrious Sean; and John Mulligan, leather merchant who was to be obituarised a 'citizen saint'. The club's objective was cultural: it had a library ('Lecky, Carlyle, History of the Magyars', etc.), there was a night school, the subjects including Irish; and members were encouraged to fish and play golf and cricket. Today the club has a football team, a concert room, facilities for darts and snooker, and three bars. The club is also open to the ladies, but only as guests.

Philanthropy, however, provided many opportunities to ladies in the superior classes to occupy their leisure hours. Their efforts were chiefly directed towards succouring children and helping fallen women to regain their feet. Scattered through the city were several creches. For example there was one in Powers

Court, off Lower Mount Street, where very young children were fed and minded for a penny a day while their mothers were out at work. Management was by a committee of ladies who required the mother to provide a certificate from the employer or from a clergyman to prove that she actually was out at honest work.

This creche had been founded in 1884 under the patronage of Dublin's cardinal-archbishop, Edward McCabe, and was conducted in a manner satisfactory to him. Although his official palace was in Rutland (Parnell) Square, the cardinal preferred to live in the modest dwelling in Kingstown (Dun Laoghaire) which he had occupied when parish priest there. But one institution in Kingstown was a thorn in his Eminence's side, the lyrically named Bird's Nest in York Road. This 'Home for neglected children of the very poor' was also managed by a committee of ladies who operated under the Irish Church Missions, which was London based and whose full title was The Society for Irish Church Missions to the Roman Catholics. To be eligible for the Nest, fledglings had to be over seven years of age as well as destitute, and the management blandly announced that 'The children of mixed marriages and of Roman Catholics are given the preference, as they are ineligible for many other institutions.'

Not many of the cardinal's youthful flock were purloined by the keepers of the Bird's Nest, but of course he would have regarded even one as one too many. The cardinal and his clergy, and their successors, inveighed against the Nest, and the faithful were instructed to cross to the other side of the road as they passed it, although at the same time uttering a prayer that the purloined nestlings would be somehow saved from perdition. In its most prosperous days the Nest used to shelter nearly two hundred children, and it survived into the first half of our century before perishing from inanition and having its solidly built premises turned into offices.

It can be mentioned in passing that although Cardinal McCabe wasn't able to get rid of the Bird's Nest, other endeavours of his in the Kingstown parish were blessed with success. The choirboys in St Michael's Church were notably well behaved, as his Eminence personally flogged those guilty of the slightest lapse from grace. But, being a humane man, he would then gently stroke their afflicted buttocks as he explained, in accordance with Victorian custom, that the punishment had hurt him more than them. Not all the choirboys were to bear malice. One, James Glover, later musical director at Drury Lane Theatre, actually boasted in his memoirs, *Jimmy Glover His Book,* of the distinction conferred upon his anatomy by the cardinal's cane.

6

Several institutions existed for the reforming of whores, the titles of which, in deference to Victorian reticence, combined coyness with essential information: for example, St Patrick's Refuge at Crofton Road, Kingstown (founded 1798) offered 'poor girls an opportunity of repairing the past by a virtuous and penitential life. Admission is obtained by applying at the Refuge, and promising amendment.' Penitence, or a profession of it, was essential at all the institutions. The St Mary Magdalen Asylum for Female Penitents in Donnybrook, run by the Sisters of Charity, who exacted, for admission, 'an assurance on the part of the candidate that she is in earnest in wishing to reform'. The somewhat more merciful Sisters of Mercy claimed that at their St Mary Magdalen's Asylum in Lower Gloucester Street, 'The inmates come and remain of their own accord.' Other titles included the Prison Gate Mission, the Magdalen Asylum, the Dublin Midnight Mission and Female Refuge Home, the Asylum for Penitent Females, and the forbiddingly named Dublin Female Penitentiary in Berkeley Place on the North Circular Road (Object: 'The religious and moral improvement of the women, and their advancement in habits of order and industry . . . all must conform to the rules of the house.')

The Dublin by Lamplight Institute at Ballsbridge (founded in 1856) showed its practical good sense by laying less emphasis on the efficacy of its redemptive efforts than on the largeness of its laundry and the goodness of its drying grounds. For at all these asylums and refuges not only souls but shirts and sheets were laundered, enabling the well-heeled city wives to frolic lawfully at night on bed linen made snow white by the penitent labours of their erring sisters.

Some efforts, though considerably less strenuous, were made to keep the men of Dublin to the straight and narrow. At No. 45 Molesworth Street laboured the Dublin White Cross

Association whose object was 'Purity among men. A chivalrous respect for womanhood. A higher tone of public opinion in the matter of purity.'

For a century and a half a familiar Liffeyside refuge was the Mendicity Institution, the popular name for the Association for the Prevention of Mendicity. This was founded in 1818 'to check mendicancy by providing subsistence for the casual poor and for those out of employment'. There was great need for the institution at this time because the previous two years had been famine-stricken. The institution depended upon subscriptions and bequests. Its income for 1899, to select a year at random, is stated to have been £1,227, and with this sum the management committee claimed to have relieved 55,116 persons during the year. Food was given to all who sought it at the institution, although a check was kept on applicants to prevent anyone benefiting habitually. Children were sent to day schools in the neighbourhood, if possible; baths provided at nominal cost, and a Christmas dinner given every year to the very poor. The chronically destitute were sent to friends who might provide for them or to places where they had been promised jobs, the railway companies granting specially reduced fares to places within the U.K. 'The committee will not assist emigration cases.'

There was a certain irony in the choice of premises for the institution. Originally it was Moira House, Dublin home of the Earls of Moira who, by the standards of aristocratic wealth, ended up almost qualifying for relief in their former mansion.

The financial rot of the Moira family began with the man who became first Earl (1762). He damaged his resources by the extravagant way he redecorated and refurnished the mansion. John Wesley visited it in 1775 and recorded his surprise at finding a far more elegant room than any he had ever seen in England. 'It was an octogon, about twenty feet square, and fifteen or sixteen high; having one window (the sides of it inlaid throughout with mother-of-pearl) reaching from the top of the room to the bottom; the ceiling, sides, and furniture, of the room were equally elegant.'

The second earl completed the family ruin by living up to his mother-of-pearl windows both in Ireland and in England. A Dubliner by birth (although the family was Ulster) he fought at Bunker's Hill and Brooklyn, and on coming home was charged in the House of Lords with undue severity towards his soldiers. The

59

charge was later suppressed. He offended Dublin Castle by condemning the cruelty with which the '98 Rising was put down, deepening his offence by sheltering Lord Edward Fitzgerald's widow and children. In the end the authorities had to get an order from the Privy Council to have them removed to England.

Fifteen years later, when the earl was in severe money trouble, he was appointed to the lucrative Indian viceroyalty but had to resign when it was discovered that he had let a banking firm loan money to the Nizam of Hyderabad, apparently not knowing that the law forbade this.

Resignation became inevitable when it was found that one of his wards was the wife of a partner in the bank. Lord Moira, who had been promoted to Marquess of Hastings, wasn't let starve. He was appointed Governor of Malta, was seriously injured in a riding accident and died in 1826 at the age of seventy-two while on a convalescent cruise in the Mediterranean. But by then his Dublin mansion had been acquired by the Mendicity Association and stripped of its top storey (probably roof trouble) and of its finery. It eventually came under the care of the Dublin Board of Assistance as a lodging house, and in the 1960s was demolished.

6

THE POLIS AND THE WATCH

DEAD dogs and cats, ordure, puddles, mud and potholes weren't the only hazards suffered by the old Dubliner when he ventured out of doors. The muggings, purse snatchings, smash and grab raids and vandalism so much complained about in our own day, merely continue ancient Dublin practice. Not that Dublin was any different from other cities in other countries, and was probably better off in this respect than London.

So long as Dublin remained a small walled city with everyone known personally to everyone else, there would probably have been little serious street crime. No doubt pockets were picked and purses cut and people knocked down and robbed if they ventured out late into the unlit streets on their own. But this kind of thing would hardly have been so widespread and on so large a scale as to be a cause of great terror to the city. There would also have been the rioting and fighting which is often the result of drunkenness, but such occurrences would have been regarded more as natural than criminal. A few extracts from the parish records of St John's church (it used to stand a stone's throw from Christchurch) paint the picture for us (the original spelling is preserved.)

> *24 November 1765:* Sheriff Rutledge and the high constable took up tow righeters in Fishamble St. with tow naked swords, they were brought to the Watch-house, and then to goal.

> *1 February 1766:* A parsell of ritters fell on James Standis on the Blind Quay, broke his lanthorn, cutt his pole in several places with swords and hangers. They all made their escape.

But it's to be noted that on 9 March following James Standish (his final *h* restored) came out on top.

> James Standish charged John Finch for nocking him doune in the street, and breaking his lanthorn, but by the consent of both partys said Finch left a crabitt and silk handkerchiefe in the constable's hands to make good the damadge.

But Watchman John Richey found his duties too much for him. On 26 May 1766 we learn that

> Between 2 and 3 of the clock a parcell of reiators armed with sword and sticks cutt John Richey in Fishamble Street in several parts of his body, and threw his pole in the river, which pole was got again and the riaters escaped.

On 24 March the following year a terse entry records:

> John Richey gave up his pole, coat, and lanthorn; he will watch no more.

On St Patrick's Day 1767 there were

> From 1 of the clock to almost 3 above 20 solgers rambling about ye parish with their naked hangers.

Yet the soldiers weren't unremittingly belligerent.

> *30 May 1767:* One Patt Conway and two solgers fell out with other in Fishamble Street, and charged each other; they forgave each other.

Nor were Dublin's women always accorded the chivalrous treatment which is their due.

> *3 July 1767:* There was one Mary Keough, an oyster woman, charged a man that would not tell his name, for makeing him open half a hundred and a quarter of oysters for him, and when all was opened and eaten he was going away until she called the watch, and brought him to the watch-house untill five in the morning, but allways refused to pay her, he saying he did not call for any; thereupon the constable let them both go away.

On 3 January 1769 Mary Browne charged one Dr Murdock and Ensign Reid 'of ye 42 Regt:

for vilantly assaulting her, knocking her downe in her own house, and giving her several blows; they struck several of the watchmen with a stick, and vemently swore they would bring a parcell of soldars, tear down ye watch-house, have the lives of all ye watchmen, and have ye constable and inspector cut into griscans.

It's worth noting that in the previous century, Cromwell's 'solgers' stationed in Dublin appear to have been kept under stricter discipline. Official records of courts martial quoted in Gilbert's *History* tell how two cavalry soldiers were found guilty of the theft of five shillings and of eight shillings' worth of goods.

> It was ordered, that they should be whipt from the Mainguard to ye Gallows and backward againse to ye said guard, each of them to receive forty lashes, being first dismounted and reduced as foote souldiers into Captn Woodstock's Company.

But as the city grew in population and in size, ingress and egress being unimpeded as the walls and gates fell into disuse, conditions began to favour lawlessness. The authorities realised that leaving the preservation of law and order to untrained and often decrepit watchmen loosely organised by the local vestry was simply not enough. In 1787 a bill was enacted for 'the better Execution of the Law and the Preservation of the Peace within Counties at large.' This empowered the lord lieutenant to appoint chief constables for the baronies, grand juries being empowered to appoint sixteen sub-constables for each district. The sub-constables, who had to be Protestant, were entitled to threepence a mile for conveying from the place of arrest to the county jail everyone they took into custody. Another threepence per mile was to be paid to members of the public who assisted them, provided that these too were Protestant.

The introduction of public remuneration for the new 'polis' (as Dublin pronounced the word), with the added benefit of paid expenses, was calculated to attract a better type of recruit, and perhaps it did in some cases. But the scent of cash also drew the careerist: it always does. For example, people who don't give a tinker's curse about how arts and artists survive, on getting the scent of monied arts councils, are transformed overnight into knowledgeable and voluble experts, eager to undertake the well-paid task of distributing largesse to poets, painters and novelists, aspiring or established, and to listen with kindly condescension to the appeals of others. It was in this way that Dublin got its first Director of the City Watch, John Giffard, 'the Dog in Office', of whom more presently.

Meanwhile the city wasn't particularly pleased with its new police, for we learn that in 1788 St Werburgh's Vestry declared in a resolution that the police were much more costly than the traditional watchmen and far less effectual.

In March of that year they were inspired by a sermon by Rev. Singleton Harper, curate of St Mary's, to appoint a temperance committee to watch the public houses, especially on Sundays, an indication that standards of police vigilance were found wanting. The committee pledged itself 'as good citizens, zealous to promote sobriety, industry, and the happiness of our fellow creatures... that we will perambulate the streets and lanes of this parish, in our respective turns of duty, as often as occasion may require, and particularly on the Sabbath Day; and that we will use our utmost endeavours to bring to punishment all persons whom we shall find retailing or drinking spirituous liquors contrary to law.'

The publicans for their part hotly resented the self-appointed law and order men. Inevitably there were clashes. We read that a publican in Crampton Court 'grossly assaulted' a patrolling churchwarden on 24 September 1769.

Naturally it was the police rank and file who received most of the kicks and few of the ha'pence. The men at the top had, as always, an easy time, the Director of the City Watch being not only a sinecurist but a particularly unsavoury one. John Giffard, born in Wexford in 1746 and educated at the Bluecoat School in Dublin, started his career as an apothecary, drew attention to himself by his zealous behaviour as a Volunteer during the heyday of that association in the early 1780s, and then went in for politics. As a politician he took the usual line, bellowing that he was a patriot first and foremost, that he would never do anything save for the good of his country and would therefore be a thorn in the side of the government. In other words, he was announcing that he was for sale, and the government bought him with the job of Director of the City Watch. His chief care continued to be for himself. He soon became notorious for the vigour with which he used the City Watch to defend his own house against the assaults of some College students. He next acquired control, or was given it, of *The Dublin Journal*, which he made a slavish government organ, earning for himself the nickname 'The Dog in Office'. So zealous a dog was he that he publicily insulted John Philpot Curran by having the audacity (according to Curran)

> to come within a few paces of me, in the most frequented part of the city, and shake his stick at me in a manner which, notwithstanding his silence, was not to be misunderstood.

Curran wrote to the Chief Secretary, Major Robert Hobart (later Earl of Buckinghamshire and Lord Lieutenant), demanding that Giffard be sacked. Since the Castle would not be ordered about by the likes of Curran, Giffard was retained and soon promoted, the affair petering out in a duel between Hobart and Curran in which their chief objective was to miss each other.

In 1794 Giffard was appointed High Sheriff of Dublin and in that capacity entered a protest against Henry Grattan's vote in the 1803 election. Grattan leaped on his high horse.

> Mr Sheriff, when I observe the quarter from whence the objections comes, I am not surprised at its being made. It proceeds from the hired traducer of his country — the excommunicated of his fellow-citizens — the regal rebel — the unpunished ruffian — the bigoted agitator. In the city a firebrand — in the court a liar — in the streets a bully — in the field a coward. And so obnoxious is he to the very party he wishes to espouse, that he is only supportable by doing those dirty acts the less vile refuse to execute.

Giffard's retort was a lame 'I would spit upon him in a desert', which does little to bear out his reputation as a skilled public speaker. He died in 1819. One of his sons became Chief Justice of Ceylon (now Sri Lanka), another was editor of the *St James Chronicle* of London and later first editor of *The Standard*. A grandson was the celebrated Lord Halsbury, long serving Lord Chancellor of England and supervisor of the digest, *The Laws of England*.

65

2

The 1787 Police Act proved to be so unsatisfactory in practice that another had to be passed in 1792 'for regulating the Office of Constable, and for the better enforcing the Process of Criminal Law in certain Parts of the Kingdom'. The men appointed under the Acts were known at first as baronial constables and later as 'old Barneys' after Barney McKeown, one of the best known of them. They had no uniform, were largely unsupervised and could follow their normal trades as well. Clearly they wouldn't have had much effect as preservers of law and order. It's recorded that one old Barney loaned his search warrant for stolen timber to a comrade in another area who used it in his search for stolen turnips.

More legislation was enacted in 1814, empowering the lord lieutenant to appoint immediately to any disturbed county or city a chief magistrate, chief constable and fifty sub-constables. Since all the local magistrates had to report to the chief, and since he was granted money to pay for private information which he hadn't to return receipts for, there was not only the temptation for chief magistrates to become autocrats but to perpetuate the unrest which had led to their appointment in the first place.

One suspects that something of this attitude lay behind the activities of the best-known and most feared Dublin law enforcer of the nineteenth century, Major Sirr. The 'major' was short for town major. This was a post connected with law enforcement for which there was no precise job specification: it became pretty much what the holder chose to make of it. Henry Charles Sirr (1764-1841) was a Dubliner by birth but English by blood. The family had a tradition of military service, which Henry Charles followed. One of his postings was to Gibraltar, where he came across Lord Edward Fitzgerald, later to be fatally wounded by him. (Sirr's Dublin school, which was run by the brothers Edward in Droppings Court, off Golden Lane, was later to educate another famous captive of the Major's, Robert Emmet.) Sirr retired from the army in 1791 with the rank of captain and set up as a wine merchant in Dublin. Five years later, when the perennial threat of a French invasion arose once more, he joined the local volunteer defence force and almost immediately was appointed its adjutant.

The city had ten companies of Volunteers, mostly traders and professional men, who naturally would have had more interest in preserving the public peace than in playing at soldiers. But Sirr was different. He found Volunteer work so congenial that he decided to make it his new way of life. The wine shop was sold and Sirr became a full-time professional guardian of the peace, leaping to prominence in 1798 by his dramatic capture of Lord Edward Fitzgerald.

Lord Edward, like Sirr, a retired army officer, was a restlessly energetic and discontented younger son of the newly created Duke of Leinster. Lord Edward saw himself as a great national leader — indeed *the* national leader — once he had succeeded in reconstituting Ireland as a republic on French revolutionary lines. Theobald Wolfe Tone saw his own future in much the same light, but in 1798 more public attention was focused on Lord Edward the duke's son than on Tone, officially the son of a coachbuilder. (He was probably the illegitimate son of one of the Wolfe family of landed gentry seated at Forenaghts in Co. Kildare.) The oppressed majority saw Lord Edward through rose-coloured spectacles as a man apparently prepared to sacrifice a great position (how little they knew, the duke's younger son might have wryly remarked), to endow them with a lot of the world's goodies with no effort on their part. To the compact and highly organised minority already in possession of the goodies, Lord Edward was the irresponsible rocker of the boat in stormy weather, a man dangerously unbalanced, a traitor to his class. Wolfe Tone, in so far as the general public was aware of him, seemed less menacing. A more shadowy figure than Lord Edward, the public had no way of realising that he was by far the abler man, and therefore the more dangerous. He appeared no more than that familiar type: the have-not who had failed to secure a good job in the public service and was now trying to cut corners to attain personal eminence and affluence through revolutionary violence. Thus Major Sirr's arresting of the bold Lord Edward in thrilling circumstances fired the public imagination, making him a benefactor or a villain according to your point of view.

But Sirr had not been first on the scene for the capture. Two of his underlings, Captain Ryan and Major Swan, had burst in on the sleeping Lord Edward in his hiding place at the top of a feather merchant's house in Thomas Street. Lord Edward drew a dagger, seriously wounding the police officers, and might have escaped had Sirr not run up the stairs and shot Lord Edward's dagger arm. (Incidentally there seems to be no end to the number of daggers which Lord Edward stabbed Ryan and Swan with. I've come across half a dozen or so in my time, at least two being included in the auction of the contents of Carton, the Fitzgerald family seat at Maynooth, Co. Kildare.) In old age Sirr described his own part in the incident in a letter to Captain Ryan's son. He told how Captain Ryan was clutching Lord Edward's legs and was about to be stabbed yet again when Sirr fired

> — and the instrument of death fell to the ground. Having secured the titled prisoner my first concern was for your poor father's safety. I viewed his intestines with grief and sorrow . . .

As well he might have done, for Ryan died of his wounds and Lord Edward would have faced a charge of murder as well as treason had he not himself died of Sirr's wound, which turned gangrenous while he was lodged in Dublin's Newgate Jail.*

3

Sirr's capture of Ireland's No. 1 public enemy/friend brought him so much attention that it turned his head for a while, or perhaps turned it a little more than it already was. His 1798 activities included the virtual theft of a valuable mare from a Dublin brewer named Hevey who was presently despatched to Kilkenny to stand trial on a trumped-up capital charge. Hevey was duly sentenced to hang. But the lord lieutenant, the conscientious and honourable Marquess Cornwallis, when examining the report of the trial before signing the death warrant, was struck by the infamy of the whole proceedings, squashed the sentence and had Hevey released. Hevey threatened legal action against Sirr for the recovery of the mare and frightened the Major into settling out of court.

In 1801 Sirr and Hevey exchanged hot words in the coffee room of the Commercial Buildings in Dame Street. Sirr arrested Hevey and vindictively had him held in a small room in the Castle where over a dozen other prisoners were already lodged

*A plaque on the site of his mother's seaside villa at Blackrock, Co. Dublin, alleged that Lord Edward died in London, the writer evidently assuming that the Newgate Jail in -question must be the notorious London prison.

in loathsome conditions. Sirr, having made the arrest in his rôle as police chief, then refused Hevey bail in his rôle of magistrate. The comment of an officer of the guard, an Englishman, was: 'If this were in England I should think this gentleman entitled to bail, but I don't know the laws of this country. However, you had better loosen those irons on his wrists, or I think they may kill him.'

Sirr compounded this disgraceful proceeding with a perjured response to a writ of habeas corpus, alleging that Hevey was in custody under warrant from General Craig on a charge of treason. The misled judge naturally refused to order Hevey to be freed and the unfortunate man was kept in custody in 'the horrid mansion of pestilence and famine', as John Philpot Curran called it in the ensuing legal action until Hevey signed a sub-mission to Sirr. After his release Hevey launched proceedings against Sirr for assault and false imprisonment, but wasn't able to be present at the hearing because he was doing a month in Newgate for assaulting another man in a pub. Nevertheless the jury found for Hevey, awarding him £150 damages.

Later Hevey was revealed to be an ardent supporter of Robert Emmet, from which we can reasonably infer that however wrong he was in his actions Sirr was right in his suspicions. However, the dancing in the streets after the verdict was announced indicates what the general attitude was to the town major.

Next to Lord Edward's capture, Sirr's best known exploit in this line was his capture of Emmet in a lodging house in Harold's Cross in circumstances that verged on the comic. He also had a few other notable arrests under his belt: that of John Sheares, the now forgotten Howley (who shot the Keeper of the Tower at the Castle), and the Thomas Russell who is often thought of as an Ulster insurgent but was in fact a Corkman. Sirr was given £500 for capturing Russell. The authorities rated Emmet as worth no more than £300.

So far as can be judged at this distance in time, Sirr's character was flawed by a tendency to crude bullying. It was said that he ostentatiously paraded through the streets with half a dozen thuggish aides, the citizens nervously making way for him. Anyone loitering near Exchange Court where Sirr had his office, and where screams and shrieks were supposed to be heard while suspects were helping the police with their enquiries, was told to clear off 'if he didn't want to find himself inside'.

69

Another story tells of a father with a ne'er-do-well son who at length so exasperated the father that he decided to have him taught a terrible lesson. He sent word to Sirr that the lad had information about certain disaffected persons which he might be 'persuaded' to impart. The lad, who in fact hadn't any such information, was picked up and without being charged with any offence was interrogated by Sirr and his aides with a cat-o'-nine-tails until he was a hospital case.

Castlereagh paid a handsome tribute to Sirr:

> The services Major Sirr has rendered to the King's Government since I have been in office [Castlereagh was Chief Secretary at the time] are such as to make me feel it an incumbent duty to bear testimony, in the strongest terms, to his merits. . . . The metropolis was peculiarly indebted for its tranquility to the unceasing activity of Major Sirr.

Although we have no hard evidence to support all the allegations about Sirr's practice of arbitrary arrest and questioning under torture, the authorities seem to have had reservations about him and his methods. In 1808 there was a further reorganisation of the Dublin police. The scheme had been drawn up by the Chief Secretary, Sir Arthur Wellesley, later Duke of Wellington, as one of his last official chores at the Castle before departing for Portugal as a first step towards settling the Napoleon problem for once and for all. The future duke, although a devout believer in discipline and public order, and convinced that nothing is more dangerous than immunity from punishment, wasn't the man to approve of Sirr's rough and ready methods. Sirr was stripped of his powers as town major, although he was allowed to retain the title and his position as a police magistrate. His humiliation encouraged Watty Cox, one of the many disgraces to the craft of journalism produced by Ireland, to launch an onslaught on him in the *Irish Magazine* (the 'Monthly Asylum for Neglected Biography'), a campaign of innuendo and character assassination that lasted until 1815 when Cox was silenced by a governmental handout of £400 and a pension of £100 a year, plus a ticket for America.

Sirr, like many other men, mellowed as he aged. He used to hold a special court very early on Monday mornings so that weekend roisterers who had been picked up for being drunk and disorderly could appear, pay their sixpenny fine and get away to be in good time for work. The Major's reduced duties left him time for his hobbies. He was an antiquary, an archaeologist, a collector of rock specimens, fossils, curios and relics. (He is alleged to have added to his collections in his police heyday at the expense of suspects.) He campaigned for the preservation of the Irish language and was a founder member of a Gaelic society. But he seems never to have lost his aggressive manner. When he attended a funeral at St Werburgh's, where Lord Edward's body lies in a vault, someone remarked to him, 'I suppose you can't be here without thinking of Lord Edward.'

'In actual fact, my friend,' Sirr retorted, 'I was wondering where you derived such an ample supply of soiled shirts.'

A favourite anecdote tells how, when rock for the building of the harbour at Dun Laoghaire was being conveyed in rail wagons from the Dalkey quarries through a special cutting, the Major was so engrossed in collecting mineral specimens from the cutting that he didn't hear a train coming and was nearly killed. The guard managed to apply the brake in the nick of time. When the workmen heard that Sirr's life had been saved they first tried to lynch the guard and, having failed, went out on strike.

Sirr died from what would appear to have been pneumonia in 1841, aged seventy-seven, at his official home within the Castle and was buried in St Werburgh's only a few feet away from Lord Edward. This was merely coincidence. Sirr went into the traditional family grave. Lord Edward had gone into his vault forty-three years previously as a temporary measure until public order was restored and the remains could be decorously transferred to *his* family burial place at Maynooth. But as often happens, the temporary arrangement became the permanent one.

4

The success of Robert Peel's metropolitan police force for London (1829) caused his scheme to be extended to the whole of England and Wales. It was only a matter of time before Ireland too had its 'bobbies' or 'peelers', although their founding father in Ireland was the legendarily efficient Under-Secretary Thomas Drummond. According to Drummond's eventual successor, the no less efficient Thomas Larcom, Drummond found on taking up his post in 1835 that the constabulary were woefully inefficient.

> By his power of organisation, and administrative skill, he converted it into the most efficient police in Europe. It became under his hands an almost perfect machine, which, like a delicate musical instrument, responded at once from the remotest part of Ireland, to his touch in Dublin Castle.

Compared with the eighteenth-century Dublin Watch and the semi-official constables of pre-Drummond days, the capital's police from 1840 onwards may well have been like a delicate musical instrument in responding to the touch of government. For the most part their everyday work would have consisted of dealing with petty crime and minor civil offences. The police statistics of the period reveal that a substantial and oddly constant number of convictions were for drunkenness. For example, in 1862, out of 25,015 summary convictions by the magistrate, 11,269 were for drunkenness. To take another year at random, 1877, the figures were 12,301 out of 40,617. For 1886 the figures were 12,699 out of 49,012. In each case the number of females convicted was about half that of males.

The increase in the total number of convictions may indicate an increase in police efficiency. The one thing it does not relate to is the variation in the city's population which, with its ups and downs between 1841 and 1901, doesn't follow the normal nineteenth-century pattern of urban increase. The population figures are: 1841 (232,726); 1851 (258,361); 1861 (254,513); 1871 (246,326); 1881 (249,602); 1891 (245,001); 1901 (290,638).

The published Dublin police statistics, however, don't reveal the main preoccupation of the force during most of the second half of the nineteenth century: the Fenian threat. Neutralising the menace of the Fenians became big business for aspiring policemen of that era.

The Fenians were founded by a few survivors of the ripple of revolution caused in Ireland by the great European upheaval of 1848. The ripple was, militarily speaking, as farcical as Emmet's rising forty-five years earlier, its Waterloo being met with in the Widow MacCormack's cabbage garden in Ballingarry, Co. Tipperary, where the insurgents fled at the approach of a detachment of mounted police.

72

Some of the '48 leaders were sentenced to share Emmet's fate but the government, in an unusual onset of common sense, commuted the sentences to transportation to the Southern Hemisphere, a relatively mild form of penal exile which enabled several of the transportees eventually to achieve distinction in public life. Other '48 men managed to get to the USA where they adopted insurgency as an interesting alternative to honest toil, declaring that they would wipe out the disgrace of Ballingarry by running the British tyrant out of Ireland.

The revived insurgents called themselves Fenians, a name which echoed that of the legendary Finn MacCool and his invincible warriors. One of the US Fenians, James Stephens, emerged as a capable and imaginative organiser and propagandist. He was a master of public relations and intrigue, with a certain sardonic humour and a truly Irish sense of the dramatic. He built up the Fenians into a vast secret organisation which, like so many of modern Ireland's semi-state bodies, was impressive in all respects except in actually doing what it was set up to do. For the Fenians were to repeat the fiasco of Ballingarry at Tallaght, although to give James Stephens his due this was because they acted against his advice. Stephens' touch of genius was to keep his Fenians in the misty background, appearing to be about to strike, no one could say where, but never actually striking.

Far from the Fenians' failure to strike making the movement absurd as the years passed, the continuing threat magnified its power and influence. The beginning of each year in the 1860s was marked by terrifying rumours that *this* would be the year of the long awaited rising, in which the whole political and social structure of the country would be overturned and the meek would inherit the earth, or so at any rate would those among them who had the foresight to join the Fenians. Dublin, being the seat of government, was especially vulnerable, and therefore especially jittery. The more astute police officers weren't slow to exploit the situation. They made a meal out of every scrap of information that came from their suspiciously communicative spies, and they worked on the nerves of the senior administrators until these worthies started seeing Fenians under every bed.

The junior administrators didn't lag behind the police. One of them, Robert Anderson, a son and brother of Crown lawyers, hung around the Castle without actually being on the staff, and hurried breathlessly along corridors, carrying sheaves of documents and looking careworn, until he managed to secure an unauthorised lease of an unoccupied desk in an obscure corner; after a decent interval he edged himself on to the payroll as a future Great Investigator. (Anderson was to end up as a big-wig in Scotland Yard, investigating the dynamite scare of the 1880s and the Jack the Ripper murders with even less success than he had with Fenianism, and supplying *The Times* with enough bad advice and misinformation to land them in the soup at the Parnell Commission.)

Another of his ilk was John Mallon, who came to Dublin from his native Armagh, joined the police and presently cast himself in the role of Great Detective, specialising in uncovering Fenians. Like Anderson he humbugged his superiors, letting dozens of shadowy figures be seen slipping in and out of his little office at dead of night, thus creating the impression that they were bringing him the very latest Fenian news.

But when he did get a tip off about a planned assassination in the Phoenix Park he failed to act on it, and on a beautiful Saturday evening in May 1882 Thomas Henry Burke, Under Secretary, and Lord Frederick Cavendish, Chief Secretary, fell to the surgical knives of the Invincibles.

John Mallon ended up an Assistant Commissioner of the Dublin police. Under cover of an abrasive air of Northern independence he was an assiduous bootlicker, a daily Mass goer, and a fluent liar. Not having Anderson's knack of writing books to boost his own professional standing, Mallon got an English journalist to write him up in the newspapers as The Great Detective, the articles being later published in hardback. The abiding impression given by the volume is that the journalist was either astonishingly credulous or else perceived what he could of the life around him through a complacent alcoholic haze.

5

It was typical of Dublin that the Fenians should have had many civilian sympathisers, even amongst the 'respectable' classes where there are always a number who enjoy creating a lounge bar sensation by talking red and acting blue. Moreover, the sympathy in America was fortified by the subscriptions of those of Irish blood whose indignation over British rule in Ireland continues to be in inverse proportion to their experience of it. A small part of the money raised was used to buy arms for the always imminent rising, the rest going on those strange administrative expenses which keep organisations from UNESCO to radio and television stations perpetually teetering on the brink of bankruptcy.

The pot was kept on the boil by incidents in Ireland like the melodramatic springing of James Stephens from the Richmond Penitentiary, a feat involving the copying of prison keys and the obvious connivance of warders. Such incidents proved that the Fenians had successfully infiltrated vital public services. They also proved that the Dublin police, when assisted by informers, could pick up the elusive Stephens, but when not so assisted couldn't prevent his slipping out of the country. In short, it seemed that the Fenian blow, when if fell, would be massive and would probably rock the British Empire to its foundations.

If only the Fenians had been able to continue their bustling inactivity they could have kept Dublin Castle's nerves on edge for a long time. James Stephens, left to himself, would have continued this policy, because his 1848 experiences had shown him how really hard it was for bands of landless younger sons of small farmers, underpaid drapers' assistants, resentful junior clerks, and men with romantic notions of themselves as warriors, all without military training, to make any headway against the disciplined and properly equipped forces of the state.

Fenian recruits and volunteers did of course include a few allegedly professional soldiers but these were more of a hindrance than a help. The ending of the American Civil War had flooded the military market with cascades of overnight colonels and mushroom generals, now unemployed and eager to revive their income by taking command of the teeming multitudes of signed-up Fenians in Ireland. Stephens wouldn't have been taken in by these warriors. Such faith as he had left in Fenianism was pinned to propaganda, and not at all to inadequately armed and low-powered force.

Inevitably he was noticed by his colleagues to be reluctant to fix a precise date for the long-expected rising. The decision was taken out of his hands. The rising was ordered, a choice selection of colonels and generals being despatched to Ireland with financial matches to light the torch of liberty. The sequel proved how amply justified was Stephens's view of the situation.

75

The evening of 5 March 1867 was the time appointed for lighting the torch. By that morning the Castle authorities were reeling under the weight of the warnings they had received. Hordes of thirsty informers besieged Mallon's little office in Exchange Court with exclusive tidings of the wrath to come. Many other warnings arrived from Anon, which suggests that there may have been several essentially unwarlike Fenians who got the summons to action in the field and wanted the Crown forces to prevent them from obeying.

The not unreasonable assumption of the Crown generals was that the principal outbreak would be in the city of Dublin, where the central government machinery could be disrupted and the nationwide bureaucracy paralysed. But this was to reckon without the military genius and originality of the American generals. *Their* plan was to march their men up the hill to Tallaght where in the confusing midnight darkness they would be given arms and marched down the hill again for the grand attack on Dublin. There, of course, the army would be waiting to blow them to smithereens. If the police intervention managed to save the army this trouble it was purely by accident.

The truth is, the Fenians' bizarre plan of campaign might have got farther than it did were it not for the gross inefficiency of the Dublin police. Although the military had been placed on full alert from early in the morning, the metropolitan police likewise, nobody thought of alerting the county police stations until the afternoon. The suburban and county officers were ordered to man the stations and reinforce certain positions. So in the dusk of a March evening a few small detachments of police set out across country to take up their positions. As it happened, an officer and two constables bumped into a band of Fenians escorting a cartload of arms to the assembly point. In the darkness the three police challenged the Fenians. A scuffle ensued during which, probably by accident, a Fenian was bayoneted. The rest fled and the horse and cart were brought to the station at Tallaght.

Here the three policemen were reinforced by a few other wandering constables until they totalled fourteen. These now resumed their nocturnal ramblings, in the course of which they again accidentally bumped into Fenians, this time the main Fenian force. Anticipating the Gilbertian police in *The Pirates of Penzance*, the fourteen constables called upon whoever was out

76

there in the dark to yield in Queen Victoria's name. The surprised Fenians, assuming that Queen Victoria's forces were at least five miles away, fired their muskets. Having only fourteen unseen targets they scored no hits. The fourteen, having at least some hundreds of targets and probably thousands, did better. The shrieks of the wounded in the darkness, the confusion, the lack of training and discipline, and the terrified assumption that the entire British army was massed against them, had its inevitable effect. The 'bold Fenian men' of the oft-sung ballad turned tail and fled, leaving their weapons scattered on the roadway.

A lot of the fleeing Fenians were picked up by other rambling policemen, and legend has it that in the weeks following the debacle some who had found refuge in the hills were hunted down with packs of hounds by the unspeakable Sir Hugh Rose, Commander of the Crown Forces in Ireland, and his staff. The torn remains of victims savaged by the hounds were slung into old quarries, sandpits and bogs. There is of course no sure proof that this really happened, but in Rose's case it isn't wholly incredible. Rose, later Lord Strathnairn, was the Indian Army officer who had had the leaders of the Mutiny blown from the mouths of cannon guns.

What we do know for certain is that the captured Tallaght Fenians were paraded through Dublin minus their braces and belts, so that they had to hold their trousers up as they shuffled along to the jeers of the Dublin crowd.

It may appear strange that after such a fiasco the Fenian threat should continue to be taken seriously for so many years. But the fact is, as already mentioned, Fenianism had grown into a profitable industry for smart operators on both sides. In America a fat living was to be got out of collecting dollars to free Ireland. Therefore reports of the Fenian Rising were faked to create the impression that the Tallaght *affaire*, for instance, was a bloody encounter between a huge Fenian army and massed forces of the crown. 'Even the elements were against us,' moaned the Fenian apologists, claiming that the night of 5-6 March had been marked by unprecedented blizzards, hurricanes and snowfalls. (The official meteorological reports say no more than that it was a cold night with some wintry showers. And anyway the weather would have been the same for both sides.) The Fenian legend, too lucrative to abandon, had to be sustained at all costs.

The same sentiment fired the bosoms of the Castle's anti-Fenian department. The plausible Anderson, recognising that London offered an even richer ground for cultivating his speciality, had himself seconded there to join the Home Office team of Fenian experts. He played the espionage game convincingly enough, his star spy being an English born and bred adventurer named Beach who, repackaged as Henri Le Caron, persuaded the American Fenian leaders that he was a French idealist eager to make Queen Victoria and her imperial lackeys bite the dust. Le Caron supplied Anderson with reports, characterised by Desmond Ryan as 'extremely cruel', about

> the youthful high spirits of Clan na Gael, its bear-garden conventions, the clash of personal vanities, the wrangling and hair-splitting and flourishing of revolutionary haloes, the Masonic mummeries and Tappertit antics.

Back in Dublin John Mallon continued to thrive as the Castle's No. 1 Fenian hunter, feeding reporters with plenty of 'authoritative' copy implying that the whole fabric of the state would totter were it not for John Mallon's acumen, vigilance, foresight, energy, skills, daring and diligence. His reputation as 'the Napoleon of detectives' and 'the prince of sleuths' survived even his bungling of the Phoenix Park Murders case.

The assassins turned out to be a breakaway group of Fenians, styling themselves the Invincibles, but were vincible enough to be arrested, tried, convicted and hanged. Naturally John Mallon gave it out that they had been brought to justice by the brilliant detective work of John Mallon. But in a book of memoirs published five years after the Mallon volume, the author, John Adye Curran, K.C, awarded the credit to John Adye Curran because of his brilliant examination of witnesses at a secret inquiry into the affair that he had been appointed to conduct. The clash of evidence between the Napoleon of detectives and the prince of interrogators makes amusing reading, and you can draw your own conclusion from the fact that Mallon didn't challenge his opponent's version.

Curran, the son of a Dublin criminal lawyer who had married a Yorkshirewoman, was one of three divisional magistrates for the city. He was appointed to head an inquiry into an assault on a Dublin juror and in the course of his investigations became convinced that the people who attacked the juror had also murdered Cavendish and Burke. He therefore requested the lord lieutenant to extend his commission to enable him to inquire into these murders, which of course Mallon had already been investigating without success.

Mallon claimed it was he who had secured Curran for the inquiry, rather improbably alleging that his superiors had consulted him on the matter. His lofty recommendation had been that of the three magistrates one was too conscientious and too dignified, another was insane, but the third, Curran, was 'sensible'. In this comical wrangle between the detective and the magistrate, Curran was the subtler combatant. He praised Mallon's detective work while contriving to leave the impression that the Napoleon of detectives merely retrieved the birds Curran shot down. The Bench does not love uppity policemen.

Probably neither was solely responsible for cracking the Phoenix Park Murders case. Each could have profited from the other's skill, but neither would have got far if it hadn't been for the informers. Nevertheless Curran is the more credible in describing his own part in the proceedings. He contradicts Mallon's claim that Mallon alone asked the questions during the secret inquiry, declaring that it was himself who did this. It's unlikely that he would have let the detective play him off the stage in his own production, or that as a skilled and practised cross-examiner he would have let a layman in this department take charge of the proceedings.

6

All in all the Dublin uniformed and plain clothes police showed themselves to be unremarkable practitioners whose lack of skill and enterprise was covered by the fortunate fact that there was little organised serious crime in the city for them to contend with. After 1867 Fenianism was largely confined to the USA, where its chief activity was fund raising for the usual imprecise objectives. The metropolitan police, having little need to show their teeth, had ample opportunity to be popular, and to conceal their almost total inferiority to Scotland Yard in every department.

Somebody got the bright idea of recruiting for service in Dublin only burly specimens of more than six-foot stature, who, being countrymen, were fresh faced, slow moving, amiable looking and almost cuddly. Known quite fondly as the DMP, they had a brass and reed band which was worth its weight in gold as an image-maker. The band performed on Sunday afternoons in a small natural amphitheatre in the Phoenix Park known as The Hollow, and generally had an appreciative audience.

But police inefficiency was once more embarrassingly exposed in 1907 when the jewels of the Order of St Patrick, known by the inflated name of Crown Jewels, were stolen from the Bedford Tower of Dublin Castle, under the very noses of the Force. To add to the comicality of the situation, the loss wasn't discovered until the eve of King Edward VII's arrival to open the International Exhibition at Ballsbridge.

Dubliners enjoyed colourful descriptions of the furious royal reaction to the loss. Edward was supposed to have shaken his viceroy, the timid and much henpecked little Lord Aberdeen, like a terrier a rat, and to have threatened the survival of his testicles should the Jewels not turn up pretty quickly. The police went on failing to uncover any clue as to how and when the Jewels were abstracted from their safe, which had apparently been opened at leisure with a key a considerable time before the theft was noticed. Since the loss didn't really affect the public there was no outcry against the police, just a lot of goodnatured bantering about the dimwits in blue who sauntered around the city, hands clasped behind back, shouting at urchins who clung to the tailboards of horse drawn carts.

A detective seconded from Scotland Yard rather late in the day wasn't able to make much progress, and was delicately headed off in a safer direction when he stumbled on the fact that a number of suspects in the case, connected with the Castle, appeared to be homosexuals. The official guardian of the Jewels, Sir Arthur Vicars, Ulster King of Arms (chief herald) and a genealogist of distinction, was made the scapegoat and was forced out of his job. The identity of the thief or thieves was never officially uncovered, but Vicars was convinced (with some reason) that it was a brother of the Antarctic explorer Sir Ernest Shackleton, and he alleged as much in a part of his will which a judge ordered to be suppressed. As is usual in such cases, there is no shortage in Dublin of illicit copies of the suppressed part.

A rumour persisted in the city for several years that the

80

Viceroy and Lady Aberdeen could have thrown light on the matter had they so desired. Indeed one of their family was unjustly named as the culprit, no iota of evidence being produced in support. But then the Aberdeens, although they unashamedly adored their viceregality, were by no means adored in return either by the Castle bureaucracy or by the public in general. He was disliked for his supposed parsimony (the family was supposed to be very hard up). She was distrusted as a do-gooder, in particular for her zealous campaign against TB, then a great scourge of Ireland. Jokes about her making personal collections of microbes began to be accepted as statements of fact, the snobbier members of society making them the excuse for not attending the levees. A popular piece of contemporary doggerel summed up much of the public attitude to the viceregal couple:

> Sez Lady Aberdeen, 'I'm next below your Queen
> Who lives across the sea and loves you dearly.
> I love you just as well
> And among you I will dwell
> For the paltry sum of twenty thousand yearly.'

The Aberdeens' unblushing request to be continued in office long after the normal term of duty had expired didn't do them any good either in Dublin or in London, and the 1916 Rising was made an excuse for making them go.

As they drove through the streets on their way to the boat, Lady Aberdeen standing up in the carriage to take photographs of the crowds (the pictures were to be shown around later as proofs of popularity), urchins yelled after them 'Dere dey go, microbes 'n' jools 'n' all!'

7

The police weren't let forget their failure to recover the Jewels, for the urchins were fond of creeping up behind them and shouting, 'Didja not get dem Jools yet?' before agilely disappearing down an alley. The truth is, if ever the Dublin police were held in high esteem it certainly wasn't during the first two decades of this century. The good effect on their image created by the excellent police band which performed in The Hollow in the Phoenix Park and on suburban bandstands, was lost during the 1913 lockout when the amiable looking giants of the Dublin

Metropolitan Police proved that their ranks included an alarming number of sadistic thugs.

But if the police hoped that they could be like the marauding dogs which return home after ripping out the throats of sheep to become once again apparently harmless pets, the hope wasn't realised. At least not so far as Dublin's working class was concerned. For when, during the Troubles, policemen were cold-bloodedly shot in the back as they patrolled the streets on duty, there was much less real sense of public outrage than one would expect.

The situation cannot justly be said to have changed much under Home-Rome Rule. The DMP uniforms were abandoned and an attempt was made to change the image by changing the name to Civic Guard. But the nuance of 'civic' went unappreciated because the effects of the essentially military training of the police remained too obvious. To this day there appears to be far more stress on 'Hup! two three four!' than on psychology at the Garda Training Depot at Templemore, and far too many of its graduates continue to treat *de haut en bas* the public they profess to serve.

It has yet to be realised that policing is one of the fine arts of governing.

7

JUDGES, MURDERERS, AND HANGMEN

1

LIKE NECESSITY, most of the Irish judges knew no law. But then they didn't have to. Ninety-nine cases out of a hundred in the Irish courts didn't (and don't) call for finely cut decisions upon knotty legal points but upon estimations of the balance of probabilities in the evidence, and the exercise of the balance of personal taste in considering the submissions of opposing counsel. Whatever the English practice, in Ireland judges were appointed more on their political than on their legal record.

Until the mid-eighteenth century the judges, like the bishops, were sent over from England in accordance with the jobs-for-the-boys tradition. Occasionally a native barrister or clergyman with useful family connections made it to their respective Benches; and a recognised path for the natives to the judicial Bench was gradually established. You ate the required number of dinners at one of the London inns of court, were called to the Bar, returned to Ireland and got yourself elected to the College Green House of Commons. There you had your choice of harassing the government until they bought you over, or adroitly using your vote until you were rewarded with a Law Officership.

The Attorney-General had the right of succession to the next chief place on the Bench that fell vacant. If the reigning Chiefs seemed in robust good health a desponding Attorney-General might accept a puisne judgeship on the half-a-loaf principle. Most of them held out. The turnover on the Bench is those days was quite brisk since its members tended to over-eat and over-drink themselves into premature apoplexy.

The Irishman's love of malicious gossip and character assassination, and his keen eye for an idiosyncracy, ensured that a new judge was soon made into a figure of fun, the process being helped by the judge's own rapidly inflating sense of self-importance. Indeed the general standards of judicial performance and behaviour were such that when a judge did actually go out of his mind the fact wasn't noticed for quite a while. Newspaper reports of the Galway Election Petition of 1872, in which the proceedings were presided over by Judge William Keogh of the Court of Common Pleas, put it beyond all doubt that the judge was unbalanced. He stormed at counsel, insulted witnesses (including bishops and their clergy), ordered the doors of the courtroom to be locked so that no one could get in or out, then walked up and down the Bench, ranting for hours on end.

It took some years for the authorities to realise that Keogh was suffering from General Paralysis of the Insane. Too late he was urged to go for treatment to a German asylum. At Bingen-on-the-Rhine, after attacking his valet with a razor, he turned it upon himself and so perished.

In fairness to him it should be recorded that in spite of shameless trimming while on his climb to the Bench, and crudity of behaviour there which was a throwback to the worst of the previous century, Keogh in his prime displayed a certain intellectual power which raised him above some of his colleagues. He had agreeable personal qualities, including humour and a disposition to do little kindnesses, which attracted warm friendship. Father Healy, an Oscar Wilde of the remoter Dublin suburbs, thought highly of him and left an affecting description of his grief at the death of a young daughter.

2

Dublin's earlier judges included many whose abilities, albeit modest, were like Keogh's obscured by the reputation as oddbods thrust upon them by the Bar and the gossipmongers. Notable amongst them was 'Copperfaced Jack,' officially John Scott, Earl of Clonmell and Lord Chief Justice of Ireland.

Scott, born in Co. Tipperary in 1739, shot up in the world quite literally. It's said that whenever he found a colleague blocking his path to promotion he picked a quarrel and shot him in the resulting duel. (This tale is told about other Irishmen of the law.) He harassed his way in parliament to the Solicitor-Generalship, remarking to the viceroy as he accepted the post, 'You've spoiled a fine patriot, my lord.'

John Scott is alleged to have laid the foundation of his considerable fortune offering to hold land in trust for confiding Catholics who were debarred from doing so themselves by the Penal Laws. The moment they signed the transfer, that was goodbye to their property in reality.

Scott eloped with the widowed daughter of a wealthy landowner, augmenting his fortune with hers and becoming owner of 21,000 acres of land in seven counties. Not long afterwards the eloper sat in judgment on a couple of youths who had followed the ancient Irish custom of forcibly abducting heiresses and marrying them against their will.

Abduction was the great social nuisance of the period. Scott broke its back by refusing to let juries bring in their customary sympathetic verdict of not guilty (the penalty for the guilty was hanging). In March 1779 he bullied a Kilkenny jury into a verdict of guilty and had the abductors hanged. After this, abduction lost much of its charm.

Scott's status at this time was that of temporary judge. He was to experience a few ups and downs in the course of the next five years but in the end was appointed Lord Chief Justice and raised to an earldom. His ambition was to attain the Chancellorship, but he never did. The post went to a hated rival, Black Jack Fitzgibbon, Earl of Clare, promoter of the Union on this side of the water.

Scott is said to have gone on swindling people even after becoming Lord Chief Justice, a practice most lawyers gave up on ascending the Bench even in those days. In fact he was about to be sued in his own court by a victim when he died, although we can be sure he wouldn't have been at all embarrassed by adjudicating in his own case and finding in his own favour.

In his own department John Scott, or Lord Clonmell as we should now be styling him, was an able man. His diaries show that he could view himself and his doings with sardonic detachment, and his frequent good resolutions, even when Chief Justice, to try to learn some law, are rather touching. He likewise resolved again and again to eat and drink less but grew so fat that his carriage springs broke under his weight. In the end he became too heavy for his own legs and had to be carried up stairs by a team of footmen.

He died at fifty-nine on the eve of the 1798 rising (the Dublin wags saying that he had chosen the time to suit his own convenience, as he always had done), and was buried in St Peter's church in Aungier Street. But he was not to enjoy eternal rest there. In the 1860s the church was replaced by an undistinguished piece of Victorian architecture which had a steadily diminishing congregation. After a century of existence the 'new' St Peter's became redundant and was demolished, its stone dressings being used to renovate Christchurch Cathedral. The remains in the churchyard were removed to Mount Jerome cemetery, so where precisely the bones lie of Copperfaced Jack and Black Jack Fitzgibbon, no one knows.

Incidentally, Lord Clonmell was the first notable person to build in Harcourt Street. His originally magnificent house still stands, although now divided into two. The larger part, later the first home of Sir Hugh Lane's Municipal Gallery, is now the headquarters of an advertising agency. *Sic transit.*

3

One of Lord Clonmell's colleagues, the silver tongued and rather endearing old judicial ne'er-do-well Barry Yelverton, the first Viscount Avonmore, was for twenty years Chief Baron of the Exchequer Division at the Four Courts. As a native of Co. Cork he enjoyed the birthright of being charming, fluent, sociable and subtly pushful. Nevertheless, for a Corkman on the make in Dublin he got through his money at an astonishing rate. His salary could be equated to a tax-free £100,000 a year in modern terms, yet he somehow managed to be perpetually in debt.

He had the itch to build big and beautiful, indulging himself with a country mansion, Fortfield, just beyond Terenure, which was famous for its plasterwork and was reputed to have Dublin's largest drawingroom. (The house was demolished in the 1930s and its grounds built over.) Other Four Courts Chiefs managed to live in similarly grand style without going bankrupt, and the mystery remains of how Lord Avonmore got through his income.

He liked telling how his fondness for meat led to his advancement. When he came to Dublin as a young man he was obliged to take a menial job as school usher. The schoolmaster's wife fed him only on bread and milk, reserving the morning bacon and evening steaks for her spouse. The deprivation goaded the

Two views from O'Connell Bridge, looking north along O'Connell Street *(above)* and south *(below)* along the line of D'Olier Street on the left and Westmoreland Street on the right. At the end of Westmoreland Street the porticos of Trinity College *(left)* and the old House of Lords *(right)* face each other.

An eighteenth-century view of the fashionable north side of St Stephen's Green, known as Beaux Walk.

Lord Charlemont, the 'volunteer earl'.

The old Tholsel *(above)*.

Leinster House *(below)*.

College Green in the early
nineteenth century showing
Daly's Club *(left)*, the old
Parliament House *(centre)* and
Trinity College *(right)*.

Peter Turnerelli's bust of Henry
Grattan, 1774-1820.

The Custom House, designed in the 1790s by James Gandon, the finest classical public building in Dublin.

Barry Yelverton, Lord Avonmore.

Dublin Castle in the eighteenth century *(above)*.

Black Jack Fitzgibbon, Earl of Clare.

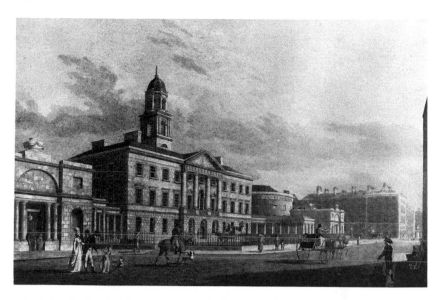

The Lying-In Hospital, better known as the Rotunda *(above)*.

The actual rotunda, seen below along with the 'new rooms' (now the Gate Theatre) was a place of public entertainment designed to generate funds for the hospital.

A modern view of the north side of Merrion Square.

Sir Joshua Reynolds'
portrait of 4th Earl
Fitzwilliam.

Two bastions of the old Protestant
interest in Ireland.
Trinity College *(above)* seen in an
early nineteenth-century painting.
John Beresford MP *(left)*
member of a family which
dominated the Irish administration
for generations.

St Patrick's Cathedral *(above)*, seen before the nineteenth-century restoration which has left it as it stands today. This was the building as its most famous Dean, Jonathan Swift *(right)* would have known it.

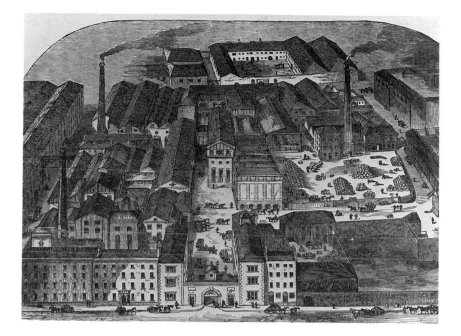

The earliest known view of Guinness's brewery, made in 1867.

The parish church of All Saints at Raheny built by Sir Benjamin Lee Guinness on the edge of his St Anne's Estate.

Victorian Dublin. The inner suburbs of Dublin's south side are as emblematic of the city as the great Georgian squares. 38 Elgin Road *(above)* was the home of Judge William Keogh. The photograph below shows a house in Kenilworth Square, one of the developments inspired by William Wellington Bentley.

The National Gallery of Ireland in Merrion Square, showing the statue of William Dargan, the railway engineer, which stands in the grounds.

The Shelbourne Hotel, St Stephen's Green, in the early twentieth century.

A shop front in Foxrock *(right)*, the area which William Wellington Bentley ruined himself in trying to develop as a weekend retreat for well-to-do Dubliners. Instead it became one of Dublin's most luxurious outer suburbs, while Bray, Co. Wicklow *(below)* became Ireland's version of the classic Victorian seaside resort.

ravenous usher into furious study of his law books, and even when at the Middle Temple recollection of that bread and milk could stave off any inclination to go slack.

Lord Avonmore was master of the dignified style of oratory, a style which appears to have impressed Dublin juries, for he was accounted the ablest advocate of his time. On the Bench he developed a habit of getting one step ahead of counsel and impatiently interrupting them. His bosom friend and fellow Corkman John Philpot Curran decided to teach him a lesson.

Curran arrived late in court one day, explaining to Avonmore that he had just witnessed a most horrowing incident. 'On my way to court I passed through the market . . . '

'Yes I know,' interrupted Avonmore, 'the Castle Market.'

'Exactly, the Castle Market. And as I passed near one of the stalls I beheld a brawny butcher brandishing a sharp gleaming knife. A calf he was about to slaughter was standing awaiting the death stroke when, at that moment, a lovely little girl came bounding along in all the sportive mirth of childhood. Before a moment had passed the butcher had plunged his knife into the breast of —'

'Good God! the child!'

'No, my lord, the calf, but your lordship often anticipates.'

As the years passed, Avonmore's financial state worsened. Even his salary was mortgaged, and he was on occasion pursued by bailiffs. When the Lord Chancellorship fell vacant he knew there was no use applying, although he did venture to beg for the Chief Justiceship. The application was contemptuously turned down.

Naturally he had little to leave to his heir to support the title of Viscount Avonmore; and his great-grandson, eventually fourth viscount, was revealed by the Yelverton Marriage Case (1861) to have descended to very shabby subterfuges to keep afloat.

4

Whatever Avonmore's deficiencies, he was still a cut above Robert Day, a Kerryman who sat in King's Bench from 1798 to 1818. Dan O'Connell's verdict on him was that although he had a good heart and would do much to serve a friend, yet 'as a judge they could have scarcely placed a less efficient man upon the Bench'. Curran declared that Day's efforts to understand a point of law resembled an attempt to open an oyster with a rolling pin.

Although devoted to his first wife, Robert Day didn't scruple to make her personal maid, Moggy Fitzgerald, his mistress. Moggy was a Catholic but considerately brought up her two sons as Protestants like their father. (They became clergymen like their paternal grandfather.) Moggy's unsevere Catholicism made Day a supporter of Emancipation, although when his wife died and he married Moggy he still went to the Protestant church in Bray on Sunday mornings while she went off in the opposite direction to the chapel at Cabinteely.

The family grave was a compromise: the old graveyard at Monkstown, where Day lies with Mary and Moggy, in peace, let us hope.

Amongst the compulsive judicial jokers, some, like Emmet's judge Lord Norbury, are alleged to have exercised their wit tastelessly during murder trials. Contrary to popular belief, Norbury's conduct of the Emmet trial was a model of decorum, and the reports don't bear out the charge that he needlessly hectored and bullied the prisoner during the famous speech from the dock.

One of the Norbury anecdotes tells how he complained at dinner that the beef didn't seem to have been well hung. 'Your lordship has not tried it,' said Curran. When Norbury in a burst of joviality invited some casual acquaintance to come and stay with him at his country house, and to bring his wife as well, he expected never to see the man again. But the man and his wife did arrive one afternoon in a cab laden with luggage suggestive of a prolonged visit. Norbury dealt with the problem neatly. He rushed down the steps, grasped the visitor's hands and said: 'I cannot begin to tell you how delighted I am to see you and your lovely wife. How charming of you to call . . . and now I insist — I really insist — I'll not take no for an answer — you simply have to stay to dinner.'

Standish O'Grady, Avonmore's successor as Chief Baron, has enjoyed a much better press for his jokes than Norbury. A Limerick man, he is said to have had a thick regional accent which, when he arrived in Dublin, he defiantly made thicker. His quips were very variable. For instance, his brother caught a boy stealing turnips and enquired if the lad could be prosecuted under the Timber Acts. 'Not unless the turnips are sticky', was the reply.

Perhaps the thick accent assisted the humour.

Rather better was his refusal to order the immediate release of a highway robber who had been perversely found not guilty by the jury. Explaining that he himself had to set out for Dublin as soon as the court rose, he said, 'I'd like to get a good start of him on the road.'

O'Grady is also credited with the remark, after another acquittal, 'You are now free to leave the court without any stain on your character except having been acquitted by a Limerick jury.' When a boy was charged with stealing a trousers and the theft was proved up to the hilt, an army of witnesses testified fervently to his excellent character. O'Grady's summing up was concise if completely out of order: 'Gentlemen, the prisoner is clearly an absolutely honest boy. But he stole the trousers.'

Charles Burton, an Englishman who was appointed to the King's Bench in 1820, was regarded as the soundest lawyer in Ireland. Be that as it may, he was responsible for depriving the Irish race of what would appear to be a natural right to fish the country's rivers. He wasn't the judge on this occasion, but junior counsel to Curran. They had been retained on behalf of a Cork landowner whose estate bordered the River Lee. There was an ancient oyster bed nearby, which the landowner claimed the exclusive right to dredge. Another man, asserting his right to take oysters from any part of a navigable river, sent in a hooker to dredge for them. The landowner distrained the hooker, and the court was asked to decide whether the sole and exclusive right to fish in a navigable river could be held as an appendant to an estate adjoining it. The case called for delving into crown prerogative, the rights of the subject in navigable rivers, and the nature of incorporeal heriditaments, the research and preparation of the submission all being the work of Charles Burton, although the actual presentation was Curran's. The landowner won his case, since when riparian landowners have never looked back.

Burton didn't enrol as a law student until he was twenty-eight, and wasn't called to the Bar until he was thirty-two. He was appointed to the King's Bench at the age of sixty, where he served with distinction for twenty-seven years. The last notable trial in which he took part was the state trial of Daniel O'Connell for sedition, and it was he who pronounced sentence of a year's imprisonment. He was eighty-four at the time, and may not have been altogether aware of the irregularities in the proceedings which caused them to be quashed on appeal to London. The appeal judge, Lord Denman, made a withering remark which has passed into history: 'Trial by jury itself, instead of being a security to persons who are accused, will be a delusion, a mockery, and a snare.'

Let us take leave of Charles Burton, however, by recording that he seems to have been the first to lay down what has proved a most useful judgment for the general public: that the language of wills and deeds and acts of parliament is to be interpreted in the grammatical and ordinary sense of words, not in the metaphysical senses invented by lawyers in pursuit of lucrative litigation.

As there was no statutory retiring age for judges in those days, many of them hung on until they almost literally dropped off the Bench. Francis Blackburne, Lord Chancellor, ignored all hints from the government to make way at eighty-four for a younger man. He offered as proof of his mental vigour that he walked to the Four Courts every day during the session, hail, rain or snow, from his home in Rathfarnham Castle, some four miles away. When he was eighty-five the pressure on him to go became too heavy and he went, protesting to high heaven about the injustice done him. He died that same year, 1867, his family declaring that the government's shabby treatment had killed him.

His judicial contemporary, Thomas Langlois Lefroy, remained on as Lord Chief Justice until almost ninety, unmoved by the ridicule excited when his son, an MP, begged to be excused from committee work in the Commons on grounds of age and it was pointed out that the father was still sitting at the Four Courts. Not even when old Lefroy had to be prompted with the words of the formula when passing a death sentence could he be shifted. Only when he was seen to be sleeping right through a murder trial and couldn't, when challenged, produce his notes of the proceedings, had he to go.

Lefroy's successor, James Whiteside, was a man of imposing stature who, as a clergyman's son, had inherited the knack of uttering piffle in unearthly tones. Whiteside's unearthliness was caused by his nose being long and blunt like a sheep's, thus imparting a cavernous resonance to his bass baritone voice.

Not only was his nose sheeplike, his whole head was. He had small bright watchful eyes, a tight straight mouth, a balding forehead of ivory skin, and hair which curled on the nape of his neck. It might be assumed that when he donned his legal wig he would look so completely sheeplike that nobody in court could keep a straight face. That assumption was corrected in my own case when I observed how solemn, even noble, was the expression of a grazing sheep, how like a judge excogitating a knotty point of law it was when raising its head and munching. Since then I've had no trouble in understanding why Whiteside's sheeplike tone and aspect caused him to be regarded as one of the greatest orators of his day.

Whiteside was a wow with juries and built up a tremendous practice. He married the sister of a colleague, the Belfast born Joseph Napier, known throughout Dublin as Holy Joe on account of his hypocrisy and sanctimoniousness. At first the rivalry between the brothers-in-law was friendly enough. They even consented to dwell near each other in Mountjoy Square. But as they advanced in their profession a certain tartness crept into the relationship , ending in hearty dislike. Napier won the race to the top by securing the Chancellorship in 1858, Whiteside having to wait another eight years before getting the Chief Justiceship.

In spite of disliking each other, the two men continued to holiday together with their wives, usually at some English watering place. Once when in St Leonard's-on-Sea, Napier, then in his late sixties, exercised his Northern humour by bribing a hotel servant to pin little bells to the underside of the Chief Justice's hotel bed, and inviting friends to listen at the door. Whiteside, another sexagenarian, took the wind out of their sails by bouncing up and down on the side of the bed for a heroic length of time.

Whiteside was the first to die. Holy Joe appointed himself chief mourner at the graveside in Mount Jerome cemetery, sobbing vociferously and fainting theatrically in the mortuary chapel. It was noted that Holy Joe became increasingly cheerful during his remaining years, even when wiping away what was intended to be a tear at every mention of 'poor Jim'. He died, aged seventy-eight, one December day in the Royal Victoria Hotel in St Leonard's-on-Sea, scene of the bells episode, and was brought back to Dublin to rest in an overground vault in Mount Jerome — but well away from poor Jim. The inscription says of Holy Joe:

An earnest and humble Christian, he consecrated to the Master's service the rare abilities he possessed, and after a long life spent in advancing the interests of Justice, Learning, and Religion, he was summoned to the nearer and holier service of the Church above.

It is pleasant now to be able to turn to a judge of that period, Francis Alexander Fitzgerald, who was in fact as honourable and upright as Holy Joe claimed to be.

5

While making his way at the Bar Fitzgerald was so scrupulously independent that he got the reputation of being too touchy. He once sent back a valuable brief because he suspected that friends had brought pressure to bear on the solicitor to offer it to him. Moreover he declined to go for parliament, devoting himself wholly to his profession and astonishing solicitors by coming into court with his brief wholly mastered. His conscientiousness paid off. When it became obvious that here was a man who always had his case carefully prepared, he was deluged with work. He had to curtail his hours of sleep and keep himself awake with large amounts of snuff so that he could labour through the night.

In one case where he found that he had tendered a wrong opinion to a client, he made good the loss (several thousand pounds) out of his own pocket.

Most of his practice was on the equity side, but his reputation for quirky honesty caused another quirkily honest man, William Smith O'Brien, leader of the 1848 rising, to engage him as his defence counsel to the charge of treason. There was little that Fitzgerald could do for O'Brien, the evidence against him being overwhelming. Fortunately, the government had no intention of hanging O'Brien or any of the others, the sentences being commuted to penal servitude. (In fact, shortly afterwards, an Act substituted transportation for certains treasons hitherto punishable by death. The Fenians were to be tried under this Act.)

In 1859, Fitzgerald, then fifty-three years of age, accepted a seat in the Exchequer Court without having applied for it or having allowed any influence to be exercised on his behalf. He thus became one of the few Irish judges appointed on merit alone, without having astutely used a parliamentary vote.

On the Bench he remained his own naturally humane and gentle self, never becoming a 'character' or acting the bully or jovial man of the world. His tenderheartedness caused his colleagues to arrange quietly that he should never have to preside over a murder trial, so that he was probably the only judge of his time never called upon to pronounce a death sentence.

As he held that it was against the public interest for a man to be promoted from one judicial office to another, he declined an offer of the Chief Justiceship, although in his case it *would* have been in the public interest for him to have accepted, since this important post passed in succession to a Belfast fool and a Galway bosthoon. The government next offered him a Lordship of Appeal — but he again declined the promotion, as he did once more when offered the Lord Chancellorship.

If ever there was any doubt that Francis Alexander Fitzgerald was unique among Irish judges, that doubt vanished after his principled stand against the 1882 Coercion Act. This Act enabled the government to set up what are now known as special criminal courts, the judges sitting without jury to try offences against the state. Fitzgerald was one of several judges who protested that these special courts would only lower the dignity of the Bench. But when the Act came into force only Fitzgerald resigned. The others stuck to their jobs.

He survived for another fifteen years, dying in 1897 at the age of ninety-one.

6

In any properly civilised country, Mr Justice Philip Cecil Crampton of the Queen's Bench would have been chucked off it with ignominy on account of the disgraceful way he conducted, in 1852, the trial for murder of a Dublin artist, William Bourke Kirwan.

Kirwan and his wife Maria were to all appearances a comfortably married couple. They occupied part of a spacious house in Upper Merrion Street, but spent the late summer months in lodgings in one of the little fishermen's cottages at Howth.

The couple used go over to Ireland's Eye quite often, he to sketch, for he was a professional artist, she to bathe. She was described as a fine figure of a woman, and about twenty-nine years of age. A happy couple to all appearances, although their

Howth landlady later testified that she heard them quarrelling in their room one evening, both the furniture and Mrs Kirwan being knocked about a bit. But such is married life, especially when circumstances confine it to a small room in a fisherman's cottage, which must serve as a bedsitter for two.

On 6 September, the day before they were due to return to their home in Merrion Street, they paid their last visit to Ireland's Eye.

Mrs Kirwan told the boatman who ferried them across to collect them about eight o'clock that evening. When he and his crew returned for them Kirwan was found alone and apparently willing to go back to the mainland *without* Mrs Kirwan. It seems that he had to be prodded by the boatmen into searching for her. A suspicious circumstance in itself, perhaps, but a plausible explanation would be that Kirwan was tired after his day's sketching, wanted to get home, was irritated by his wife's wandering off and not coming back in time to be taken off the island, and on arrival at Howth would have sent the boat back again to collect her.

After an hour's search by Kirwan and the boatmen, the chief boatman saw something white down on the rocks in a pool. It proved to be Mrs Kirwan's body. It was later alleged that blood was oozing from her breasts, ears and vagina, but apparently no remark was passed about this by anybody at the time. Kirwan threw himself on the body, wailing 'Maria — oh Maria — Maria.' He stayed alone with her in the dark while the boatmen went off to bring the boat around to the pool.

He insisted, when the body was brought back to Howth, that it be washed and laid out for burial, although the police had ordered it to be left alone. A medical student arrived next day, declared that death had been caused by drowning, and a local inquest jury returned a verdict of accidental death. Poor Maria was then brought to Glasnevin cemetery for burial.

But in Howth there remained a number of disgruntled persons complaining about the smallness of the gratuities handed around by the bereaved during the removal. As the days passed, the complaints became more bitter. Extraordinary allegations were made. What had hitherto been accepted as the ordinary cries of seagulls now became the last piteous shrieks of Maria as she was being done to death over on Ireland's Eye. The three women who laid out the body now became positive that the bleeding was not menstrual or the result of the body being scraped against the rocks by the tide. It had been caused, they declared, by stab wounds of a revolting nature. Kirwan's umbrella, it was confidently asserted, was really a swordstick.

The rumours filtered back to Dublin and a middle-aged woman, a neighbour of Kirwan in Upper Merrion Street, pestered the police with allegations that the artist was not only a wife murderer but a bigamist. Since she supplied the address of the second 'wife', the police went to Sandymount and interviewed a Miss Kenny, known locally as Mrs Kirwan, who admitted that she had borne Kirwan eight children. (The lawful Mrs Kirwan hadn't borne any during twelve years of marriage.)

Maria Kirwan was exhumed three weeks after burial. As the coffin rested in soggy ground it had filled with water, a circumstance which, added to the fact that the body wasn't taken away to a laboratory for examination, can hardly have helped post-mortem investigation. Of the three doctors who viewed the remains, Dr George Hatchell, physician to the lord lieutenant's household, declared that Mrs Kirwan had been strangled. The second doctor disagreed. His opinion was that she might have died in an epileptic fit brought on by entering the cold water for a swim after a meal. The third doctor was adamant that Mrs Kirwan had died from stabbing. He was a Dr Geoghegan from Baldoyle, which isn't far from Howth, so it's possible that he was influenced by the rumours put about by the fisherfolk.

Since the three doctors were agreed on one point, that the lady was dead, Kirwan was arraigned for murder and was tried at Green Street courthouse before Mr Justice Philip Cecil Crampton who, on this occasion at any rate, took leave of his senses.

The Cramptons were a prominent Dublin family who produced not only men of the law but a fashionable surgeon of a vanity remarkable even in one of that calling, and a diplomat who, when British ambassador at Washington, nearly caused a serious rupture between the two countries by trying to enlist Americans for the Crimean War. Mr Justice Crampton's contribution to the gaiety of the nation was one day to undergo a sudden conversion to teetotalism on the road to Bray, and on reaching his country house there to empty his entire cellar into the River Dargle.

Like James Whiteside he was the son of a clergyman and had

inherited the itch to address the multitude. This he eased by haunting public meetings and, irrespective of what the subject for discussion was, denouncing the demon drink and advocating total abstinence as the only sure passport to paradise. But his conduct of the Kirwan trial would have suggested, did we not know to the contrary, that he was suffering from a hangover.

The prosecution, which was powerfully assisted by Crampton, relied on Howth gossip about the row at the lodgings, the alleged screams from Ireland's Eye, and Dr Hatchell's assurance that Mrs Kirwan had been strangled. Isaac Butt, defending, was able to make mincemeat of Dr Hatchell, and momentarily impressed the jury by pointing out that one row in three months isn't bad going for a married couple, especially when they are billing and cooing again by the following morning. But the jury were fixated on Kirwan's illicit ménage at Sandymount and the prosecution scored a great point by revealing that on the day after Mrs Kirwan's death Miss Kenny and her eight children had moved into the house in Upper Merrion Street.

But the preposterous contradictions of the doctors and the obvious wildness of the rumours from Howth had planted doubts in the jury's mind, in spite of Judge Crampton's heavy summing up against Kirwan. Forty minutes after retiring, they came back with the news that there wasn't a hope of their agreeing. This seemed to throw Crampton into a rage. He told the jury they weren't really trying, and adjourned the court until eleven o'clock that night so that they could make up their minds.

When the jury reappeared at eleven, they said they still couldn't agree. Crampton retorted that they would now be locked up all night in the jury room, they could take it in turns to sleep on the wooden benches, and there would be no refreshments. (This was in accordance with the then law.) Finally, although it was a bitterly cold night, there wouldn't be any fire. He hoped they would find their overcoats warm enough.

The jury now descended to Crampton's level. They begged him to allow them another five minutes. In the event they took twenty, coming back with a verdict of guilty, to the astonishment of everyone present — except Crampton, who expressed his satisfaction. After an unpleasantly sanctimonious lecture to the accused, Crampton told him there was no hope for him in this world, donned the black cap and sentenced him to hang.

But that wasn't the end of the matter. A number of doctors and lawyers took up the case, analysed the evidence, exposing its frailty and condemning the manner in which the trial had been conducted: and, to cap all, Judge Crampton himself wrote to the lord lieutenant to urge a reprieve. The reprieve was granted, which caused the rumour to go around that the condemned man wasn't being hanged because he was related to the Chief Secretary on his mother's side.

Efforts continued to have Kirwan freed, as it was becoming increasingly recognised that there had been a grotesque miscarriage of justice. A famous forensic expert, Alfred S. Taylor, M.D., F.R.S., considered the evidence put forward at the trial and concluded that 'no murder was committed'.

> The theory of death assumed by the prosecutor is not only not proved, but actually disproved by the appearances on the body . . . I assert as my opinion on a full and unbiased examination of the medical evidence in this case, that so far as the appearance of the body was concerned, there is an entire absence of proof that death is the result of violence at the hands of another. Persons bathing or exposed to the chance of drowning are often seized with fits which may prove suddenly fatal, though they may allow of a short struggle. The fit may arise from syncope, apoplexy, or epilepsy; either of the last conditions would, in my opinion, explain all the medical circumstances in this remarkable case.
>
> It is my opinion, as the result of twenty years experience in the investigation of those cases, that the resistance which a healthy and vigorous person can offer to the assault of a murderer intent of drowning him or her is in general such as to lead to the infliction of greater violence than is necessary to ensure the death of the victim. The absence of any marks of violence or wounds on the body of Mrs Kirwan, except such small abrasions as might have resulted from accident, may be taken in support of the only view which it appears to me can be drawn, that death was not the result of homicidal drowning or suffocation, but most probably from a fit resulting from natural causes.

Matthew Bodkin, a county court judge who published a book

about famous Irish trials, quoted Taylor with approval, mentioning that Taylor's opinion was publicly endorsed by a number of eminent Dublin doctors and surgeons. Bodkin himself said:

> The case is commonly referred to as the Ireland's Eye murder. I cannot adopt that phrase. On a most careful consideration and collection of the almost verbatim reports of this extraordinary trial, published in the newspapers of the day, I am convinced that no murder was committed, that William Burke Kirwan . . . was wholly innocent of the crime.

(You will note that by a slip of pen Bodkin, having declared that no murder was committed, later refers to the 'crime'.)

But in spite of all the public agitation and the petitions, the authorities refused to free Kirwan, thus displaying their own inconsistency. For if Kirwan *was* guilty there was absolutely no reason to reprieve him, and if there was doubt enough to justify a reprieve he should have been freed altogether. The authorities seem to have been swayed by other considerations, even apart from Kirwan's flouting of Victorian 'morality'. Allegations were in the air that he had been paying £40 a year to a certain Mrs Boyer to prevent her publicly charging him with swindling her husband out of an art collection worth £3,000: that the husband had gone to stay with Kirwan and had disappeared; and that in the garden of the house where Kirwan had apartments being dug up, the remains had been found of a child in a crude coffin.

Kirwan was the last prisoner to be confined on Spike Island before it was handed over to the military. (In 1985 it was returned to use as a prison.) The sentimental story is told that on his release an aged and decrepit Kirwan paid a visit to Ireland's Eye before vanishing for ever. But according to Bodkin, the Spike Island doctor accompanied Kirwan, who was still in his fifties, to Liverpool, whence he sailed to America.

8

SCRIBBLERS, SHYSTERS, AND PUBLISHERS

1

THE Watty Cox and his *Irish Magazine* mentioned briefly in
the last chapter in connection with Major Sirr, was merely
one of the succession of gutterpress 'journalists' of whom Dublin
has always had her ample share. Cox, a Co. Westmeath black-
smith's son, born about 1770, came to Dublin as a hanger-on of
the United Irishmen movement, started a journal called *Union
Star* to be their recognised organ, was repudiated by the leaders,
went to America, and returned to start the *Irish Magazine*, which
got talked about because of its sustained campaign against Sirr.
As already related, Cox and his journal were silenced with a
governmental handout and faded from notice.

The first Dublin newspapers didn't appear until the late
seventeenth century. In 1685 *The Dublin News Letter* was printed
in College Green and published by Robert Thornton at the
'Leather Bottle' in what is now Christchurch Place. Crudely
printed on inferior paper, it came out three times a week and
lasted for at least seven months, possibly much longer. It seems
to have been intended less for home consumption than for
export to England to satisfy curiosity about what was happening
to English expatriates.

Before this there had been occasional one-sheet bulletins, containing semi-official information, a kind of rudimentary gazette.
There were also manuscript news sheets of a kind that had been
circulating in England since the sixteenth century concerning
which we can only speculate about their being the ancestors of
the modern gossip column, designed more to entertain spicily
than to inform soberly. English produced journals found their
way over to Dublin and must have been eagerly read for the
snippets of news they contained of what was happening in the
big world outside. In due course it occurred to Dublin printers

99

that there was a definite home market for a regular newspaper. The dawn of the eighteenth century saw the launching of a series of journals: for example, *The Dublin Gazette or Weekly Courant* (1703), *The Dublin Mercury* (1704), *The Dublin Intelligence* (1705) and, signs of the penal times, *The Protestant Post Boy* (1712). Most had mayfly existences. Since the papers lived by their circulation revenue, there being virtually no advertising revenue, the printers eventually found this particular game not worth the candle. Some papers which died in one man's hands were revived under the same title by another, some were kept going at all costs by people bitten by the journalistic bug. It has been calculated that during the first half of the eighteenth century 165 newspapers were started in Dublin, of which at least 120 were published by only twenty-two stationers and their families.

In England the papers must have had the same kind of powerful influence on the public as television does today. At any rate the government tried to keep them under control, first by a Licensing Act which soon became a dead letter, then in 1713 by a Stamp Act which imposed a duty of a penny on every sheet and a shilling upon every advertisement. The measure was introduced by the Tories to muffle the Whigs' press campaigns by keeping papers beyond the reach of as many pockets as possible. Needless to say the Whigs in their turn retained the duty to dish the Tories, and the duty was increased over the years until by 1815, the year of Waterloo, it stood at a punishing fourpence, which in modern terms was like having to pay £10 government tax on your morning paper and the same on an evening edition. In 1836 the duty was brought back to one penny and was finally done away with nineteen years later.

Duties imposed by Westminster didn't automatically apply to Ireland, so Ireland's newspapers escaped direct taxation until 1774, presumably on the ground that it is unnecessary to muzzle sheep, especially sheep in pastures too poor and too distant to affect the proceedings of the British parliament. Besides, conditions in Ireland imposed their own limits on newspaper circulation. The mass of the people had neither the inclination nor the means to buy papers that could influence their political attitudes, assuming such papers were available. The fact is, during the first half of the eighteenth century the Dublin newspapers were virtually non-political. Their contents consisted of 'reports' from the various European capitals, giving news of governmental doings and the results of battles anything from a week to six weeks after the event. London news was most respectfully reported. After all, the newspaper readership in Dublin was deemed to be mostly expatriate Britons anxious for tidings from the mother country. The tradition of giving generous coverage to British news in Ireland's national papers has continued to this day, although the compliment wasn't returned until recent years when somewhat cynically produced 'Irish editions' are flown over daily to justify advertising department claims of 'complete coverage of the British Isles'.

2

The advantages of owning or controlling a newspaper, being obvious, were soon perceived in Dublin. A properly handled newspaper seemed an easy path to money and power. The early Dublin newspapers were accordingly not just printers' sidelines but magnets for odd-bods: social climbers, political schemers, adventurers, life improvers, fools, idealists, time servers, blackmailers and persons combining two or more of these characteristics. John Whalley (1653-1724), who started *Whalley's News Letter* in 1714, was by trade a shoemaker who diversified into quack medicine, necromancy, astrology and yellow journalism. He survives in Irish pop history as a harmless idiot who happened to earn a contemptuous epitaph from Swift (or someone with a very Swiftean style):

> Here five foot deep lies on his back
> A cobbler, starmonger, and quack,
> Who to the stars in pure good will
> Does to his best look upwards still.

In fact he was rather a nasty customer who fulfilled a promise to provide in his *News Letter* 'a full and particular account of foreign and domestic news' by packing its pages with scandals, reckless libels on prominent citizens, fake prophecies and lickspittle support of the government. His journalistic stock-in-trade included a running No-Popery campaign (during King James II's sojourn in Ireland, Whalley had to fly to England for safety), and his frequent predictions of the downfall of the Pope and the College of Cardinals, together with the destruction of the city of Rome, seem to have been popular news items. It's hard to accept that he was taken quite seriously by Dubliners, whose long memories wouldn't have let them forget how he had been stood in the pillory for a political offence and pelted with ancient eggs. Nevertheless there's an ingrained tendency in us at least to half believe what we see in black and white in the papers, no matter how extravagant or incredible it would appear if related *viva voce*. *Whalley's News Letter* must have done great mischief in its time.

Whalley kept up a continual paper war with his colleagues, although whether the disagreements were genuine or merely got up affairs to cater for Dublin's love of public squabbles would be hard to determine.

A less unsavoury tycoon was George Faulkner (1699-1775), founder with James Hoey of the *Dublin Journal* which first appeared on 27 March 1725 and survived for almost exactly a century. The Faulkner-Hoey partnership broke up five years later, and from then on Faulkner was sole proprietor, editor and, he intimated unconvincingly, sole writer. Originally published twice weekly, four pages for one penny, it eventually came out three times a week.

The popular image of George Faulkner descends to us as a figure of fun with a wooden leg, brilliantly mimicked on the Dublin stage to the delight of his printing house apprentices by the actor-playwright wit Samuel Foote, and as the putative father of Mary Ann Faulkner, the master/mistress of the lord lieutenant. The image is inadequate and misleading. George Faulkner was clearly an excellent editor and a sound business-man.

Today's newspaper readers will be interested and/or amused to learn that the practice of printing on Saturdays pious and satisfied panels of godspeak contributed by the dog-collared, is an old as *Faulkner's Journal.* George's first number, coming out on a Saturday, opens with a sermonette by 'The Observator'. Although the text is drawn not from Scripture but from Juvenal, drone of heavenly harmony is only too familiar.

> Religion not only commands an entire Abhorrence to all Manners of Wickedness, but also commands a true and un-feigned Submission to the Law and Will of God, so that a truly good Man not only avoids the Follies of this World, and the Vanity and Wickedness of Mankind, but also lives

102

up, as far as in him lies, to the Tenor of that which is good and acceptable in the sight of his Maker.

Then, having vindicated his journal's claim to 'Being the Freshest Advices, Foreign and Domestick' with belated reports from 'Dantzick, Stockholm, Rome, Vienna, and Hambourg', George got down to real business with the 'Domestic Advices'.

> On Wednesday last, Mr Richard Nelson (who kept the Cross Keys, in Deanery Lane, leading from Cavan's* Street to St Patrick's Close), an Ale Seller, Cut his Throat. He was generally reputed a Man of tolerable sense in his own Way, but was lately observed to be melancholy, and somewhat frantick, in which condition ('tis thought) he committed this unnatural act, and made so unhappy an Exit.

And even spicier:

> And Yesterday, one Moll Mooney (God bless us!) a Nymph of the Town, confined in Bridewell for deluding (as is reported) another Woman's Husband, attempted to put an End to frequent Chastisement, by taking away her Life, in the prevailing manner aforesaid, but was prevented by the want of Courage to go through the Operation, or the Bluntness of the Knife. However, by the Scar from Ear to Ear, and the great quantity of Blood, she has not failed to let us know she was in earnest.

George Faulkner, according to his obituary notice in the *Hibernian Magazine*, was born in Dublin in 1699, the son of a butcher whose wife was second cousin to Viscount Dillon. Having been schooled by Dr Lloyd, described in Gilbert's *History of Dublin* as 'the most eminent schoolmaster of his day in Ireland', George was apprenticed to a printer, in due course entered into partnership with Hoey, and after the dissolution of the partnership went on to prosperity, an aldermanship, and the prestige of being Swift's publisher.

One of many anecdotes about Faulkner tells how he caught Swift's interest. When the printer of *Drapier's Letters*, John Harding, died in prison, Swift sent for one of the Faulkner-Hoey partners to be interviewed for the vacancy. Hoey went and

*George Faulkner's phonetic rendering of Kevin's Street.

103

when asked if he was a printer replied that he was 'an apology for one'. When asked where he lived, the answer was 'facing the Tholsel'. Swift then requested the attendance of the other partner, whose answers to the same questions were 'I am' and 'Opposite to the Tholsel'. Faulkner's purer grammatical style got him the job, and this may well have been the beginning of the end of the Faulkner-Hoey partnership.

Faulkner's *Journal* has been criticised for being too bland, too careful about not offending anyone. But in these respects it wasn't much different from other Dublin papers of the period, and an editor can hardly be charged with excessive prudence if, like George Faulkner, he was more than once hauled before parliament for daring to print critical comments on parliamentary procedure, offences he expiated whether by going to jail or going down on his knees to receive a severe reprimand.

George was evenhanded in his criticisms. In 1753 he commented in the *Journal* that modern patriotism consisted of 'eating, drinking and quarrelling', a remark which stung the patriots into lampooning him in pamphlets as a court lackey, but which shows how little things have changed in Ireland over the years.

George Faulkner wasn't the type to be bothered by a short sojourn in jail (when he could afford to make himself almost as comfortable there as at home) or by the mumbo-jumbo of kneeling for a parliamentary reprimand. He would have known that there's no such thing as bad publicity provided you can turn it to good account in your business. The news that the editor of a Dublin paper had got into hot water would certainly have done no damage to the circulation figures. Here again a Swift anecdote illustrates this side of George Faulkner's character. Swift's biographer Thomas Sheridan (the playwright's father) tell us that when Faulkner returned from a visit to London he called to the deanery, dressed like a dandy.

> Swift received him with all the ceremony that he would show to a perfect stranger. 'Pray, sir, what are your commands with me?' 'I thought it my duty to wait on you immediately on my return from London.' 'Pray, sir, who are you?' 'George Faulkner, the printer.' 'You George Faulkner, the printer! Why, thou are the most impudent, barefaced impostor I ever heard of. George Faulkner is a

sober, sedate citizen, and would never trick himself out in lace, and other fopperies. Get about your business, and thank your stars I do not send you to the house of correction.'

Many another Dubliner would have been mortally offended by the insult. But Faulkner, sufficiently established in his trade to be able to afford to tell the dean to go to hell, merely went home, changed his clothing and returned.

Swift, on seeing him, went up to him with great cordiality, shook him familiarly by the hand, saying, 'My good friend, George, I am heartily glad to see you safe returned. Here was an impudent fellow in a laced waistcoat, who would have fain passed for you; but I soon sent him packing with a flea in his ear.'

George Faulkner must have done very well out of his various editions of Swift's works, and although it was the tradition in those days that no gentleman would condescend to accept payment for work published, a tradition most scrupulously respected by publishers, Swift seems to have been well pleased with his printer. The Swift connection (and the dean was reputed to contribute to the *Journal*) gave Faulkner prestige, and Swift had the satisfaction of being published by the printer he could describe as 'most in vogue'.

A tradesman of George Faulkner's standing inevitably became a member of the Corporation, and George was amongst the aldermen. A rumour went around Dublin that he had been offered a knighthood* by Lord Chesterfield, Viceroy in 1745-6, whose special mission was to charm the Irish into neutrality during the Jacobite troubles in Scotland by liberal distribution of promises and application of soft soap. Chesterfield was credited with brilliant success in his mission, although the probable truth is that the Irish, cynically remembering the behaviour of their last Stuart hero, King James II, declined to get excited about Bonnie Prince Charlie. At any rate George Faulkner never became Sir George, but Chesterfield, even after his departure from Ireland, continued to profess the highest

---

*The Viceroy was empowered to create 'Irish knights', a lesser breed than the English variety. Irish knighthoods are regarded in London more or less as coloured beads for the natives.

esteem for the Dublin publisher, comparing him to Atticus and deploring that George should have omitted to dine with him during a visit to London.

In 1762 a visiting English actor, Samuel Foote, 'the prowling Aristophanes of our age', staged his farce *The Orators* at the Smock Alley Theatre, in which Faulkner was lampooned as Peter Paragraph. The lampooning was hardly a difficult feat since George had a wooden leg and a pronounced lisp, the result of losing teeth in a fall from his horse. Dublin had already had its unkind fun over George's wooden leg (the 'wooden understanding' of 'the man with one leg in the grave'), so that Foote's victim was in no mood to be ridiculed virtually on his own doorstep, since the Smock Alley theatre was only a few yards away from Faulkner's home and printing house in Essex Street. Faulkner would have been better advised to ignore Foote altogether. But he plunged into the kind of public squabble in which Dubliners take an unholy delight. It seems that Faulkner bought a block of seats for the show and sent his employees in to hiss it off the stage. The plan misfired, the employees laughing heartily at Foote's take off of their limping, lisping boss. Faulkner sued Foote and was awarded substantial damages, which caused Foote to flee the country.

Foote revenged himself by repeating on the London stage his impersonation of 'that little hopping fellow, the Dublin Journalman.' But the last laugh was with Faulkner. Foote himself lost a leg in a riding accident and Faulkner had the satisfaction of reporting the incident but without comment. He later allowed Foote to reappear on the Dublin stage without moving to recover the damages.

After Swift's death Faulkner launched a fund to erect a memorial but Dublin didn't bother to subscribe and the project perished. Some time later Faulkner published Lord Orrery's memoir of Swift, a memoir candid enough 'to expose to the world matters which it was thought he should, as Swift's friend, have confined to his own bosom'. The memoir, which took the form of letters from Lord Orrery to his son, dealing frankly with certain of the dean's foibles and failings, described his decline in old age with an unpleasant lack of sympathy, as if the noble lord felt that he himself would never fall into dotage. (In fact he didn't live long enough to do this, dying at the age of fifty-five). Faulkner's decision to publish the memoir may have been an error of judgment in public relations, or a belief that posterity was entitled to know all that was to be told about the dean that couldn't have been published in his lifetime. Or it may have been simply grasping at what seemed a profitable project, with Faulkner only too eager to add a well-known literary peer to his list of authors and not bothering to read the manuscript with care. (Publishers don't always have the time or the inclination to read every word they issue under their imprint.)

At any rate, Dubliners chose to make the memoir a cause of righteous indignation, the kind that would have burned brightest in those who hadn't read a word either of the memoir or of the works of its subject. Pamphleteers and epigrammatists had a field day, one neatly killing the two birds with one stone:

> What! libel his friend when laid in ground;
> Nay, good sir, you may spare your hints,
> His parallel at last is found,
> For what he writes George Faulkner prints.

The publication of Orrery's memoir doesn't appear to have done Faulkner any great material damage. It has long been quoted against him as yet another instance of his folly, insensitivity and ingratitude, but the fact remains that some of those who rap Faulkner have been eager to make good use of the memoir.

Another and more important fact remains: that if anyone has a claim to be hailed as the father of the Dublin newspaper it is George Faulkner because of his fortunate combination of commercial ability with journalistic flair. Besides, in comparison with his successors, the Dog in Office Giffard in particular, he stands as an honest and honourable man.

3

Faulkner's *Journal* had its rivals. There's little to choose between it and Reilly's *Dublin News Letter* (1731). Where the *Journal* scored was in point of longevity, although here it was beaten by *Freeman's Journal*, which first appeared in 1763 and lasted for 160 years.

Charles Lucas, the apothecary turned doctor turned political agitator and pamphleteer, who took on Dublin Corporation and the Irish parliament and had to skip the country for a while, is sometimes mentioned as the founder of *Freeman's*, but he wasn't. He was a profuse contributor of verbal assaults on public dignitaries, one of his favourite aunt sallies being the lord mayor, not just one in particular but any lord mayor. The *Freeman's* reader, on opening the paper and seeing only three columns of tedious tirade, would conclude that old Charlie mustn't be in good form today, for he usually ran to four columns. Lucas seldom signed his name to the tirades but his pen names of 'A Citizen' and 'Civis' were well known and there could be no mistaking his ungripping style. By the standards of modern journalism he was a verbose bore, but it wouldn't be fair to throw verbosity at him: the nature of eighteenth-century Dublin newspapers almost enforced it. There simply weren't enough suicides in Dublin, or abductions, floggings, hangings, murders and whorings to fill all those columns of tiny print. Charles Lucas and his like must have been a godsend to the printer in a humdrum week when there was no news, when not even his Britannic Majesty was threatening to fire his ministers or they threatening to resign, when not even the King of Prussia had won a battle nor the Empress Maria Theresa lost one.

Not that Dr Lucas had many avid readers, for no avidity could find his opening paragraphs appetising. (His 'Essay on Mineral Waters' runs to three volumes, containing in all 874 pages.) But although Charles Lucas's effusions may have been unread their existence would have reassured the apathetic public that someone somewhere was keeping an eye on supposedly important issues. And he wouldn't have been the first author or the last whose reputation and influence depended upon his not being read. After all, *The Origin of Species, Das Kapital, Finnegans Wake* and the Bible must be the most widely unread famous books in the world, yet who are more venerated by their adherents than Darwin, Marx, Joyce and God? Charles Lucas, once chased out of Dublin by the Corporation, now has his statue in the City Hall. He even survived his part in the preposterous Turkish Baths affair, of which more anon.

Freeman's Journal was launched in September 1763 by three Dublin shopkeepers, apparently as a commercial speculation. The usual claims were made for it, and hints were dropped that important personages were behind it, the three shopkeepers keeping a low profile. It was supposed to be conducted by a committee of eminence, but in fact the first editor was Henry

Brooke, bland poet, romantic novelist, and controversial play-wright. A Cavan man, he was born about 1705, the son of a well-off person who had a highly connected wife. In youth Brooke gained the good opinion of Swift, who ironically regretted 'that his talent pointed towards poetry, which of all pursuits was most unprofitable'. He went to London to study law, was recalled to Ireland to settle the affairs of an aunt who had died, leaving a 12-year old daughter of uncommon beauty. Brooke, aged eighteen, became guardian of his young niece, marrying her two years later (so much for the forbidden degrees of kindred) and over the years fathered twenty-two children upon her. Only two survived. (One was Charlotte Brooke, an enthusiast for Gaelic poetry which she collected, translated and published, together with the original text in a volume entitled *Reliques of Irish Poetry* [1789].)

At first Brooke tried to make a career in London, but although he got good reviews for his poetry and a five-volume novel was respectably received, he can hardly have been making much money. His play, *Gustavas Vasa* (1739), created a furore, its rhetoric about death to tyrants and the indefeasible rights of freemen provoking the Lord Chamberlain to ban it from the English stage. But if the Lord Chamberlain chose to see dangerous heresies in these platitudes, Dublin audiences pre-ferred to see the celebration of heroic aspiration when the piece was produced for them under the title *The Patriot*.

In 1740, Brooke having made £1,000 by the publication of the text of the play in England, returned to Ireland, where despite the bravado the *The Patriot*, he was appointed to the sinecure post of barrack-master of Mullingar, worth £400 a year. This typically Irish combination of safeness and reputed daring, making for the perfect parlour patriot, must have made him appear to the shopkeeper-entrepreneurs the ideal man to edit the *Freeman's Journal*. They must have been delighted with the first number (10 September 1763), in which readers were given the hot news in four columns that

> man comes into this world the weakest of all creatures, and while he continues in it the most dependent.... Sacred history appears to intimate that man was originally created invulnerable and immortal, the angelic lord and controller of this earth and these heavens that roll around us....

Brooke, having vaguely likened 'the quick and apparent communication of a Free Press' to 'animal spirits to a body politic of Society', couldn't resist sounding yet again the clarion call that had so frightened a Lord Chamberlain a quarter of a century before:

> Turkish tyranny hath at once plucked up liberty by the roots, in forbidding the printing of all writings whatever through their dominions. . . . we, therefore, openly declare ourselves the enemies of all tyranny, and of all sorts of tyrants, whether single or Hydras. . . .

and in deference to readers who mightn't know what Hydras were, Brooke elucidated:

> . . . the one or many headed monster.

Brooke, who had in him the makings of the perfect television investigator, concluded by allaying any niggling worries his shopkeeper-proprietors might feel about the hazards of defying tyrants nearer home than Turkey.

> We engage never to point at any breach, but in order to repair it; never to probe a wound but in order to heal it.

> > Cursed be the line, how well soe'er it flow
> > That tends to make one worthy man our foe;
> > Gives virtue scandal, innocence a fear.
> > On from the soft-eyed virgin steals a tear.

As an old hand at journalism myself, I can hear Henry Brooke remarking as he laid down his quill, 'well, lads, I think that about covers everybody and everything.'

Henry Brooke seems to have drifted away from the *Freeman's Journal* as Charles Lucas surged into it. His wife's death sapped whatever will to live advancing age had left him. His daughter Charlotte's devoted care kept him alive for a few years until he faded out altogether at nearly eighty.

As for Charles Lucas, his state of perpetual indignation seems to have worn out not only his wives (of whom he had three) but himself. A description of him in his later years, runs:

> The gravity and uncommon nearness of his dress; his grey, venerable locks, blending with a pale but interesting countenance, in which an air of beauty was still visible,

altogether excited attention, and I never saw a stranger come into the House [of Commons] without asking who he was.

But at this time he was not as you might imagine a well-preserved eighty: he was only about fifty-five. He died at fifty-eight and was given a public funeral to St Michan's churchyard. Henry Grattan the Younger, who inherited some of his father's tendency to humbug, declared that he had 'laid the groundwork of Irish liberty. Lucas was the first who, after Swift, dared to write "freedom".' The historian Lecky cast a colder eye on him. 'His pamphlets and addresses have been collected; they form one thick and tedious volume.'

Lucas, who was an M.D. of both Leyden and Dublin Universities and a member of the London College of Physicians, was one of twenty-five Dublin doctors (another was Dr Robert Emmet, father of the insurgent) who supported a proposal to build a public baths in the city. The proposals were put forward early in 1771 by a picturesque Turk, styling himself at first Mister and then Doctor Achmed, and dressing the part. Dr Achmed appears to have convinced the doctors that his baths would have valuable medicinal properties. *Freeman's Journal*, presumably with Lucas's backing, puffed the proposals, announcing that the baths could be built for an estimated £612. 4. 0d. Subscriptions were solicited. The announcement was accompanied by a certificate signed by the doctors stating that Achmed was well qualified to operate the baths. In due course the committee reported

> that they had that day viewed Mr Achmed's baths on Batchelor's Quay, and that they appeared to them very methodically constructed; that the house is elegant and completely furnished and the whole well calculated for public utility.

A further press announcement at the end of the year indicated that the baths were successful. But the success was only of the Dublin kind: it lasted only so long as the novelty lasted. First, Dr Achmed's oriental origin was challenged and in the end he was revealed to be either a Mr Patrick Joyce of Kilkenny or a Mr Kearns, son of a Dublin tradesman. Moreover, it was alleged that public funds had been granted to him to help run the baths, and that the hallowed Irish tradition had been followed whereby the parliamentarians who voted the grants for the public good were themselves the chief beneficiaries. Elegant entertainments were available to them at the baths, with no stinting of wines or spirits, and no fuss about exacting payment at the door.

4

Lucas died in 1771, and thereafter the story of *Freeman's Journal* is one of shameful decline. For a while it was owned by a rapscallion named Francis Higgins, better known as the Sham Squire. He was born about 1746 in a Dublin cellar to Roman Catholic parents who had migrated from the North of Ireland to better themselves. Higgins was by turn messenger boy, shoeblack and potboy before somehow getting a foothold in a lawyer's office as a clerk. While with the lawyer he forged a document purporting to prove that he owned an estate and was worth £3,000 a year.

He used the document to induce a Dublin merchant named Archer to hand over his daughter in marriage, although the girl was physically repelled by Higgins. And small wonder, for Higgins, as later described in a hostile ballad, was no Adonis:

> Clothed in a morning gown of many a hue,
> With one sleeve ragged and the other new;
> While obvious eructations daub his chin
> With the remaining dregs of last night's gin;
> With bloated cheek and little swinish eye
> And every feature form'd to hide a lie;
> While every nasty vice, enthroned within
> Breaks out in blotches o'er his freckled skin.

It didn't take Archer long to find out that his new son-in-law was a penniless adventurer who was being sadistically cruel to the bride. The girl went back to her parents and died shortly afterwards, as did they. But before departing this life Archer managed to get Higgins jailed for fraud. The trial judge dubbed Higgins 'a sham squire', and the biting nickname stuck. On the death of his wife Higgins promptly married the jailer's daughter and after serving an oddly short term revived his fortunes by selling smuggled tea at cut prices to the Dublin grocers whom he then betrayed to the excise authorities and collected the government reward. The Judas money was invested in brothels and gambling houses, the fat profits being used to finance loans to businessmen whom Higgins ruined by recalling the loans without warning at the most awkward moment. In this way he got hold of their property on the cheap, one of the gains being the *Freeman's Journal*. Higgins, who had now turned Protestant, offered the freedom of the *Freeman* to the government, printing their slanted news in return for lucrative official advertising. Complaints were made in parliament about the amount of public money being paid for the publication of worthless announcements, one MP pointing out that by quoting a Whiteboy manifesto in the middle of a government proclamation it had gone around the country much more effectually than the Whiteboys dared hope. It also came out in the debate that Higgins was ensuring wide circulation for *Freeman's* by distributing it gratis among the pubs.

Gutter journalism made Higgins rich, and the ex-conman who had done time now dispensed justice from the Bench as a J.P. for Co. Dublin. He moved to a mansion in St Stephen's Green where in the evenings he entertained the judiciary to sumptuous dinners after having spent his mornings in the law courts —

> He comes, and round him the admiring throng
> Catch at the honey dropping from his tongue;
> Now promises — excuses round him fly;
> Now hopes are born — and hopes so quickly die;
> Now he from b — ds his daily rent receives,
> And sells indemnity to rogues and thieves.

The verses quoted above were printed by Magee in his *Dublin Evening Post* (No. 1746) and not even the Sham Squire's pious churchgoing at St Andrew's or his ostentatious almsgiving could save him:

> The cunning culprit understands the times,
> Stakes private bounty against public crimes,
> And, conscious of the means he took to rise,
> He buys a credit with the spoils of vice.

Entertaining the judiciary must have amused Higgins not just because of his appearance in the dock but because he had earlier

113

applied to be admitted an attorney of the Court of Exchequer and had been told by Chief Baron Foster that if he dared to repeat such an impertinence he'd find himself in Newgate again. But if he failed to get the right side of the Chief Baron he did better with John Scott, 'Copperfaced Jack', the Chief Justice of the King's Bench and Earl of Clonmell. His house, a handsome mansion in Harcourt Street, had pleasure grounds on the opposite side of the street, to which one could get by an underground covered passage. The Chief Justice's gardens adjoined the Sham Squire's rear garden, and this made it handy for the two men to have a chat in privacy whenever they wished. In all probability it was the judge who encouraged Higgins to start libel proceedings against Magee and his *Evening Post*. Higgins did so, arranging for three other persons to join him: a theatre manager, a hack from *Freeman's,* and his own mistress. Incredibly, the proceedings were heard in Copperfaced Jack's court in June 1789 and equally incredibly he issued four 'fiats' against Magee marked with the impossible to raise sum of £7,800.

Some weeks later Magee enjoyed his first instalment of revenge. He leased some fields adjoining the Chief Justice's seaside villa at Blackrock, where Copperfaced Jack had spent a fortune and many years on beautifying his gardens with flowers and rare shrubs. Magee invited the public at large to come a grand fête in his fields. For the occasion asses were dressed up in judicial scarlet and full bottomed wigs, dancing dogs provided with barristers' gowns and the mob was encouraged to make as much of a racket as they wished. The grand finale was a pig chase. Magee announced that whoever could get hold of a pig could keep it. The pigs had their tails greased and were then 'accidentally' driven through the hedge into the judge's gardens where, with the help of the mob, they turned a thing of beauty into a dust heap.

It was a fiendish revenge, but who is to say the judge didn't deserve it. Magee suffered for his fête when in due course he again appeared before the judge. Higgins had engaged every leading barrister to act for him: Magee was virtually on his own and fought like a cornered rat. He explained that he had been out of town on the day one libel was published, having been entertaining citizens under his lordship's windows and seen his lordship 'peeping out of one of them all the morning'.

Magee added that the morning after the fête he had overtaken the judge as he rode back into town: 'Your lordship was riding cheek by jowl with your own brother Matthias Scott, the tallow chandler from Waterford, and audibly describing the price of fat the very moment I passed you.'

When Magee inevitably was jailed he sent the judge a note 'with his compliments' to report that his health was much improved 'since he got his heels out of Newgate'. The enraged judge ordered an immediate inquiry into how Magee had managed to get out of jail and was informed that Magee's way of getting his heels out of Newgate was to thrust his feet through the bars of the cell window. Magee's next move was the rather shabby one of hiring thugs to throw scalding water on the judge while he was in a public bath.

After many delays and a long time in custody Magee was finally brought to trial and by bullying the jury the judge extracted from them a verdict of guilty with damages assessed at £200. Magee managed to get himself jailed again for contempt of Copperfaced Jack's court but the fight was too unequal. Magee broke down and died in 1809, insane and hard up, justifying in a way, perhaps, the judge's remark during the libel action that 'it was obvious from the poor man's manner that he was not just then in a fit state to receive definite judgment.' His son, another John, continued to run the *Dublin Evening Post* on his father's lines and, like his father, ran into libel trouble. He was fined £500 and sentenced to two years but didn't live to serve it all, dying in 1814 after just a year behind bars.

Francis Higgins had enjoyed the satisfaction of silencing the most trenchant and wounding of his press attackers and, like so many men of his kind, continued his vain pursuit of respect and prestige in the city that knew his origins and his disgrace, had seen his rise and the method of it, and begrudged him every penny he possessed. He died quite suddenly at the age of fifty-six on the night of 10 January 1802 during a fearsome thunderstorm. His will was a final desperate attempt to win a good name. After legacies to friends, including his lady friend, the rest of his fortune went to charity, the Lying-in Hospital ('the Rotunda') receiving an endowment for a Francis Higgins Bed. Money was also left for a substantial monument with a laudatory inscription to be put over him in Kilbarrack Cemetery.

For more than half a century the former owner of *Freeman's*

Journal was let rest in peace at Kilbarrack until an amateur historian, W. J. Fitzpatrick, managed to get hold of the Dublin Castle secret service books and published his theory that the F. H. recorded therein as having been paid £1,000 for giving information about Lord Edward Fitzgerald was Francis Higgins. Whereupon a band of Dubliners, inflamed with patriotism and drink, hurried out to Kilbarrack with picks and shovels to dig up the Sham Squire's bones and throw them to the dogs. Finding impromptu exhumation tougher than expected, they contented themselves with smashing the laudatory tombstone. No trace of it can be identified today.

5

So far as Dublin Castle was concerned Francis Higgins served his turn and gave value for money. The Castle didn't fare so well with a later prostitute journalist, James Birch, proprietor in the 1840s of a journal he magniloquently called *The World*. The reigning lord lieutenant, the Earl of Clarendon, sanctioned the hiring of Birch and his paper to counteract the propaganda successes of the Young Ireland organ *The Nation*. In return for money, Birch, who governed *The World* from No. 7 North Richmond Street, printed the 'official' versions of public events but didn't succeed in undoing the damage caused by *The Nation* and its talented team of Young Ireland writers. Birch's services were dispensed with after he had received a total of £1,700. But he wasn't to be discarded so easily.

He drew up a list of 'services rendered' and sent it to Lord Clarendon with a bill for £7,000. The response was unsatisfactory. Birch threatened to sue for the money and Clarendon, to avoid publicity, foolishly paid another £2,000 to Birch. It was now the turn of the Chief Secretary Sir William Somerville to be squeezed, but Somerville stood his ground and Clarendon, realising too late the folly of treating with a blackmailer, resolved to stand with him. The case was heard in the Four Courts in December 1851 before Chief Justice Blackburne. The jury were told how Birch had been paid by the Castle for his support. Clarendon, waiving his viceregal privileges, went on the witness stand to tell how he had paid Birch the extra £2,000 to keep his mouth shut. Birch didn't do well in cross-examination and the result, arrived at in three or four minutes after a hearing lasting two days, was a verdict for Sir William Somerville. But as only sixpence costs were awarded against Birch the victory was hardly overwhelming. *The Nation* rubbed it in:

> Lord C, has grown most awfully religious,
> Said Corry Connellan* with a rueful air;
> At least his trepidation is prodigious
> As to how in the next *World* he'll fare

Meanwhile *Freeman's Journal*, which had hit rock bottom, underwent a remarkable revival. A Mayo-born doctor, John Gray (1816-1875) who had settled in Dublin, added politics to his medical activities. He contributed articles to *Freeman's* and eventually bought the paper. He supported O'Connell in the Repeal of the Union campaign which, when later re-titled Home Rule, was assumed by the public to represent a dramatic advance in policy. He shared O'Connell's imprisonment in 1844 for sedition but after the Liberator's death in 1847 and the inept Young Ireland Rising of 1848, he transferred his considerable energies to what he regarded as more practical objectives, while remaining a Home Ruler. His interest in chemistry and engineering, and his uncommon aptitude in mathematics, equipped him as a member of Dublin Corporation to push through against bigoted opposition the great Vartry River Scheme which for the first time supplied the city with an assured supply of pure water from a reservoir in Co. Wicklow. At the inauguration of the supply on 30 June 1863 he was knighted. Seldom has the honour been better deserved. Although Sir John Grey was a Protestant he was too much the businessman to let this interfere with his development of *Freeman's Journal* as the recognised organ of Catholic and popular nationalist opinion. The paper supported Gladstone's Irish policies and praised his plan to disestablish the Irish Church. So when Sir John died at Bath in 1875 in his sixtieth year it isn't surprising that he was accorded a public funeral to the nominally non-sectarian but in fact Catholic cemetery at Glasnevin. The burial service was read by Bernard Shaw's uncle, Rev. W. G. Carroll, rector of St Bride's, the expensive vault being given free by the cemetery authorities (to him that hath, more be added); and the widow and son raised over him a memorial that did not understate his

*Corry Connellan was Lord Clarendon's private secretary.

117

achievements. His larger than life bust was supported by a sculptured shaft whose sides are carved with four figures representing (1) the spirit of the River Vartry; (2) the figure of enfranchised religion, trampling her fetters underfoot; (3) an Irish maiden gleaning the fruits of a land blessed with security and peace; and (4) the spirit of Education, reading from a volume of learning as she points heavenwards to the even greater lessons to be learned up there.

Gray's public statue in O'Connell Street more frugally limits its praises to the water supply.

Freeman's now passed into the hands of Sir John's son, Edmund Dwyer Gray, who continued his father's policy. In 1882 he allowed the paper to publish a letter which revealed that a murder trial jury when locked up overnight in a city hotel, got roaring drunk and rampaged around the place bellowing their intention to ignore the evidence and hang the defendant. Edmund Dwyer Gray was prosecuted for contempt of court and sentenced three months and a fine of £500. 'Let Mr Gray be now taken into custody', said the judge.

The officers of the court hesitated, as well they might, for Dwyer was High Sheriff of Dublin and their boss. Since it was he who was officially responsible for taking convicts into custody, the question was: would he sweep himself off to prison? He made no move. The judge impatiently repeated his order and an officer nervously edged forward to remove the High Sheriff to the Bridewell and to new eminence as a national hero.

Six years later Dwyer virtually dropped dead at his home in Upper Mount Street. He was only forty-three, a circumstance which must have surprised those who remembered how at twenty-one he had been robust enought to rescue five people from drowning in Dublin Bay. Like his father he was ahead of his time in some ways. He astonished his fellow Irish journalist, 'Tay-Pay' O'Connor, first editor of the London paper *The Star*, by recommending him to include a sport section as a most important feature in any modern paper. When the telephone uttered its first hoarse crackles and most people saw in it nothing more than an amusing toy, Gray persuaded his board of directors to have a phone system installed at *Freeman's*, leaving other Dublin papers to follow suit years afterwards.

6

The Catholic sympathies of *Freeman's* left the Protestant badly in need of daily journalistic reassurance at the breakfast table. The need was met to some extent by the venerable and dull *Saunders News Letter* and respectable and dull *Daily Express*. The afternoon sustenance required to fill the gap between one morning and another was provided by the Dublin *Evening Mail*. Of the three the *Mail* was to last the longest, achieving a century of existence as a grand old institution which shared with the *Irish Times* the reputation of keeping two headlines permanently in type: SERIOUS CHARGE AGAINST CLERGYMAN and SCOUTMASTER ON SERIOUS CHARGE. But whereas the *Times* contrived to print such items with an air of doing a painful duty, the *Mail* was clearly offering them as interesting items in their own right, and did not shrink from including details which the *Times*, blushing, dropped in the wastepaper basket. In due course the *Mail* enlarged its repertoire to include WOMAN PATIENT ACCUSES DOCTOR: according generous space to what the *Times* dismissed in a paragraph.

The man who set the *Mail* on the path it was to follow through three generations was Dr Henry Maunsell. Born in the heart of Dublin in 1806, a son of the general manager of the Grand Canal Company, Maunsell trained as a surgeon. In 1839 he started, with another doctor, the *Dublin Medical Press*, a weekly crammed with trade advertisements which rapidly made him his fortune. In 1860 he bought the *Mail*, printed whatever local news was cheaply available and topped up the remaining space with matter lifted without payment from British and foreign papers.

Maunsell's political policy was simple. He adopted the provincial papers' practice of printing speeches by candidates at election time at a charge of so many pence per line. Editorial praise of a candidate cost a shilling a line. In my youth I was told by veterans of the press that this practice, which obviously had to be hush-hush, was continued by the *Mail* long after other big papers had dropped it, and that an extra guinea or two could be picked up by *Mail* men able to guarantee prominent positioning of the puffs.

Older Dubliners will have vivid memories of a once famous newsboy cry: 'Heggelomayell! Heggelomayell!' This, interpreted, signified '*Herald* or *Mail*', the *Herald* being the *Mail*'s more straitlaced rival, which resolutely averted its puritan gaze from serious charges and women patients' accusations. For many years Dubliners carried outward and visible signs of their religious affiliations. Soft hats, coloured shirts, imperfectly cleaned footwear and the *Irish Independent* and *Evening Herald* proclaimed the Roman. Bowler hats, white shirts, brown leather gloves, rolled umbrellas, gleaming footwear and the *Irish Times* and *Evening Mail* denoted membership of the Anglican communion.

In its later years the *Mail* was noted for printing copy more or less as received from reporters and correspondents. Court reports which in other Dublin papers were tactfully sub-edited or condensed appeared *in extenso* in the *Mail* and provided riveting reading for the prurient. The paper's letters page was a popular feature, and a recognised playground for wits and wags. Solemn protests would appear over signature like 'Soldier's Wife' against alleged orders by the Minister for Defence to have unofficial structures in Portobello Barracks dismantled and all unauthorised erections in married quarters prohibited for the future. A heated correspondence would develop over several days, being chopped only when the *Mail* discovered its leg was being pulled.

The arrival of the new bright and brash *Evening Press* in 1955 weakened the already faltering *Mail*. A few years later it was taken over by the *Irish Times*, the intention being to teach the old dog some new tricks that would make it give the *Press* and the *Herald* a good run for their money. But the many arbiters of the dog trainers didn't include that sharp eye for the dramatic which had made the *Press* a quick and lasting success, and the dog it was that died.

The *Irish Times* was the creation of a typical twentieth-century tycoon who happened to be born in the nineteenth century. He was Laurence Edward Knox, grandson of the second Earl of Rosse and establisher of the imperialist and Protestant tradition of that paper until in other times and other hands it became more Northern Irish than the Irish themselves and more clamorously sexist in the feminine interest than *Cosmopolitan* itself. (Major Knox would have approved of these developments as commercially wise.)

In youth Knox gained enough military experience to attain the rank of major and as MP for Tower Hamlets in London enough know-how to see how politics is an easy way to acquire eminence without ability, and control of a national newspaper a great provider of influence without undue effort. Knox, more a predecessor of Lord Beverbrook than a successor of Sir John Gray, may cause amateur psychologists to wonder whether in childhood he was neglected by his mother, since in manhood he was an exhibitionist who sought to buy affection with ostentatious hospitality. His town house was in Fitzwilliam Square, and for a country residence he had a former hunting lodge, Ballinascorney House, set high in the hills of Co. Dublin. This house enjoyed some fame as a place where Robert Emmet sought refuge while on the run.

Almost every week in summer Knox would fill a four horse drag with ladies and gentlemen, and bear them away up to Ballinascorney to be royally entertained for a long weekend. He had another horse-drawn vehicle carrying twenty or thirty printing apprentices, dressed in colourful uniforms and equipped with musical instruments. The lads trumpeted and drummed and piped their way to the lodge to herald the arrival of Knox and his guests. The noise, we are told, 'could be heard for miles around'.

Knox might have shaped the course of Irish journalism quite interestingly for years to come had he not died young. He was felled by scarlatina at thirty-six, leaving to the beautiful cousin he had married a consolatory £25,000. The widow took little interest in the paper. She didn't marry again, but during a long and elegant widowhood mourned the husband who, though well born, hadn't been altogether a gentleman.

The place among Dublin newspaper proprietors which Knox might have occupied fell to a human bird of prey from Bantry, Co. Cork, named William Martin Murphy.

William Martin Murphy, archetypal conquering Corkman, was born in 1844, eldest son of a contractor. He was schooled by the Jesuits in Belvedere College, emerging with a lean faced old head on young shoulders: pious, soft-spoken, ruthless; dedicating himself with unnerving single mindedness to the gathering in of power and money, every penny of which he would defend tigerishly. When he was nineteen his father died. He took charge of the family business, extending it from the usual building of churches and bridges to railway and tramway engineering. He laid tram tracks in England and in Scotland,

121

and is said to have laid the first such tracks in Buenos Aires. He built railways on the West African coast, and in Ireland was chairman or director of several major and minor railways, including the legendary West Clare. He acquired large city stores, important hotels (including The Imperial in O'Connell Street), and having gained control of the *Daily* (later *Irish*) *Independent* he founded the *Evening Herald* and, in 1906, the *Sunday Independent*, thus being the first Irish newspaper magnate to achieve the ideal of keeping the printing presses going morning, noon and night, seven days a week. He permitted the papers to exhibit a prudent nationalism, since this reflected the sympathies of the bulk of their readership. It's doubtful whether he himself had any deep-rooted political feelings, his politics being those of his class: the politics of the £. Small wonder then that Dublin viewed him with a sardonic eye:

I entered a tram and rode all day
On a regal couch and a right of way
Which reached its arms all over the land
In a system too large to understand.
'A splendid property this!' I cried
And a man with a plate on his hat replied —
'It's Murphy's!'

I went to Heaven. The jasper walls
Towered high and wide, and the golden halls
Shone bright beyond. But a strange new mark
Was over the gate, viz, 'Private Park.'
And a saint with a livery on replied —
'It's Murphy's!'

I went to the only place left. 'I'll take
A chance in the boat on the brimstone lake,
Or perhaps I'll may be allowed to sit
On the griddled floor of the bottomless pit.'
But the jeering tout with horns on his face
Cried as he forked me out of the place —
'It's Murphy's!'

As chairman of the Dublin United Tramways Company Murphy reacted as one would expect to Big Jim Larkin's attempt to enrol the tramwaymen in his Irish Transport and General Workers Union. Larkin had in fact enrolled about half the tramwaymen before Murphy made his move, which was to demand that every tramwayman sign a pledge to remain at his post in the event of Larkin calling a strike. This was in August 1913, which was rather late in the day to tackle Larkin, he having started his fight in January of that year in the docks and having become by the end of May virtually dictator of the Port of Dublin. By calling a strike at harvest time he had forced the agricultural employers to surrender, and by planning a tram strike in Dublin as Horse Show Week approached, he expected that Murphy would run up the white flag too. But each under-estimated the other's determination.

Murphy met Larkin head on. The preliminaries included an exchange of vulgar name calling in their respective papers, Larkin using his little weekly, the *Irish Worker*, to call his opponent 'capitalist sweater', 'blood-sucking vampire', 'white sepulchre'. Murphy retorted in his *Irish Independent* with 'a big man, wearing a slouch hat and with a swaggering style, throwing downstairs any smaller man than himself and giving the impression of great physical courage', 'this convicted and mean thief', and 'scum'. It's not surprising that this trading in personalities led to a personal antagonism in which the industrial and trade union issues were superseded and the matter became one of James Larkin *v* William Martin Murphy.

Murphy organised a brutal lockout by four hundred firms as the grand retort to the strike, cheerfully remarking to the Dublin Chamber of Commerce that the employers at least would be having their three meals a day. But those who assumed that the Larkinites would be quickly starved into surrender reckoned without the determination of men who have nothing left but their pride and their principles.

As the months went on and there was little sign of settlement or surrender, there must have been some firms amongst the Murphyites nervously wondering about their financial future and how long it would take them to recoup losses, just as there must have been thousands of Larkinites who felt their struggle was becoming pointless but feared to be the first to suggest the white flag. In the event the strike crumbled just before the lockout did so that Murphy appeared to have beaten Larkin into the dust. World War I, which began a few months later, distracted public attention from trade union concerns. When hostilities ceased and Europe was trying to adjust itself to the astounding news that three mighty empires had been toppled and their emperors turned into refugees or corpses in a cellar, it was noticed that in Dublin the trade union movement still existed and was gathering new strength. Larkin's defeat had been merely a victory deferred.

7

Dublin's early printers earned themselves a good name in the trade as enterprising and judicious businessmen who pirated London successes with little delay and commercial risk. Their ambition was to smuggle pirate editions into England and undercut the British publishers. The law prohibited Irish publishers from exporting their books there, pirated or not. What success they had is obviously impossible to gauge accurately but in spite of the small home market they prospered mightly. The basis of their prosperity was a highly effective method of distribution which had something in it of the Tupperware principle. They sold their publications in bulk to door-to-door bagmen (chapmen) who travelled the country, doing particularly good business with clergy and schoolteachers. Their wares were chiefly of the devotional kind, with story books and a sprinkling of the more respectable classics. Two chapmen who did very well for themselves were the Protestant Luke White and the Catholic James Duffy, of whom more anon.

The plum job in the trade was that of King's Printer. This lucky man had the exclusive right to print all proclamations and official publications of the government, also the Holy Bible and the Book of Common Prayer, official publications of a reputedly higher authority. The first of the King's Printers was Humprey Powell who, as 'Prynter for the Realme of Irelande', operated in St Nicholas Street in the latter part of the sixteenth century. But the first big achiever in this branch of the business was George Grierson, who began printing in Essex Street about 1709 and, fifteen years later, issued the first Irish printing of *Paradise Lost* and the same of Sir William Petty's famous Maps of Ireland ('the Down Survey'). Grierson's acumen extended to his choosing of a wife. Constantia Grierson (née Phillips) was saluted as one of the most learned scholars of her age. Letitia

Pilkington, whose readable memoirs don't inspire complete confidence, tells us that Constantia was 'mistress of Hebrew, Greek, Latin, and French; understood the mathematics as well as most men; and what made these extraordinary talents still more surprising, was that her parents were poor illiterate country people; so that her learning appeared like the gift poured out of the Apostles of speaking all languages, without the pains of study...'

George Grierson published several of his wife's works, including a three-volume edition of Tacitus which was spoken highly of. She was admitted to Swift's circle and was said to have innocently vamped the lord lieutenant, inspiring him to couple her name with her husband's when Grierson's patent was renewed, so that technically she ranked as the only woman to be a King's Printer. A pleasant story, but Hugheo's list of Patentee Officers in Ireland cites only her husband's name. Constantia, who was nearly thirty years younger than George Grierson, died at twenty-seven, leaving an only child, a son, who was praised by Dr Johnson as possessing 'more extensive knowledge than any man of his years he had ever known.' The son died, like his mother, at twenty-seven.

The Griersons held the office of King's Printer for four generations, developing a passion for building mansions in the Dublin foothills, renting others, and never staying long in any. It was a Grierson who built the lodge at Ballynascorney later occupied by Major Knox. There was a huge boulder in the grounds into which Grierson inserted the romantic but dubious statement:

> Finmacoon, one of the Irish Giants, carried this stone on his shoulder from the opposite Mountain on April 1st 1444 — he was 9 feet 7 inches high, and 44 stone.

Eventually this restless Grierson moved a few miles away to another hillside to build the house known as Mount Venus, the grounds of which were embellished with a cromlech of more genuine ancestry than 'Finmacoon's' stone. Mount Venus features in one of the romantic chapters of George Moore's *Hail and Farewell*, but has been reduced these fifty years to no more than a few bits of wall. Grierson's next move was merely a few hundred yards further down the hill, where he built Woodtown House. But political changes put a stop to his building frenzy. The Union having brought a big reduction in government printing, Grierson was compensated, and is said to have put the money into farming and cattle breeding at Woodtown and ruined himself.

Another Grierson eccentricity was to maintain six complete dinner services, each being left dirty until all had been used. There was then a big washing up, and the cycle started again.

The other Royal Printer who left a notable mark on Dublin was Alexander Thom, who flourished in Victorian times and was therefore Queen's Printer. He was the son of a Scots immigrant who had somehow managed to steer his printing business onto the rocks. The father had favourably impressed Sir Robert Peel when Peel was Ireland's Chief Secretary. Years later, when Peel was Tory leader at Westminster, Thom junior asked him for some government printing. Peel munificently responded by getting Thom the contract for all the Irish Post Office printing, thus making Thom's fortune.

Thom, having good reason to praise the Lord, compelled his employees to do likewise. The employees, who put in a 65-hour week, paid by piecework, had to start their day with a prayer of thanksgiving for having been spared to see another day, with a second outburst of prayer for the welfare of Alex Thom who so kindly provided them with work remunerated at under six old pence per hour. They prayed of course in their own time.

Thom's contract included the printing of the Post Office Directory. Other Dublin printers were already in the market with street directories, an almanac 'and general Register of Ireland'. But in 1844 Thom issued a larger, more comprehensive, more orderly and altogether more useful directory which wiped his rivals off the map and survived as a national institution for a hundred and thirty years. By then the cost of producing some three thousand minutely printed pages of names and addresses, with an index, bushels of statistics and lists of every possible kind, had, because of high printing wages, become prohibitive. The directory struggled fitfully on under new management for a couple of years, the standard of preparation and presentation dropping far below old Thom's, and then expired ingloriously.

It need hardly be said that Alex Thom hated and feared trade unionism with its 'perpetual menace of illegal combination.' Not that this made him unique in his time. He had more apprentices than qualified printers (24 and 22 respectively), the apprentices' pay rising to ten shilling for their 65 hour-week in their seventh and final year. In other words, a substantial part of Thom's Directory was produced by child labour. Yet strange to say Thom was regarded by his employees as rather a decent old skin.

8

Alex Thom wasn't the only Scotsman to do well out of Dublin printing and publishing. James M'Glashan, who came to Dublin from Scotland early in the nineteenth century, started on his own in D'Olier Street and then muscled in on William Curry Junior and Co., printers and booksellers in Upper Sackville (O'Connell) Street, eventually becoming the managing partner. In 1833 half a dozen TCD graduates started a magazine aimed at the general public but with the off-putting title of *Dublin University Magazine*. It filled a gap which in Scotland was already filled by the famous *Blackwood's Magazine* and four years later was to be filled in England by *Bentley's Miscellany* until that publication was put in the shade by the magazines edited by Charles Dickens. After six months the graduates sold out to Curry's. It took quite a long time for M'Glashan to grasp that the *DUM* contributor with most readership appeal was a Dublin born medical practitioner then working as a dispensary doctor in the North, Charles Lever. M'Glashan decided that Lever was well worth exploiting, and did this by paying him enough to give up doctoring and come back to Dublin, and by generally taking over his life.

The trouble with Lever was that he ate too much, and, before the onset of middle age, was physically too restless to be a dependable magazine hack of the kind M'Glashan required. M'Glashan's trouble was that he wanted to run everybody's life but lacked the charm and tact and grace of manner that might have enabled him to do this without causing intolerable offence. Like many of his fellow countrymen he was a brainy barbarian, even more repellant in his openhanded moods than when miserly, and he had the ability to get through a bottle of whiskey a day while remaining convinced that he was almost a tee-totaller. (He was a member of a once famous Dublin dining club, The Mystics, really a carousing club, which met at the Bailey Tavern in Howth.)

The runaway success of Lever's *Harry Lorrequer* and *Charles O'Malley*, serialised in the *DUM*, made the author a valuable asset. M'Glashan must have realised that sooner or later Lever would be coaxed away by British publishers, and met the problem of how to pay Lever more without upsetting the magazine's usual rates by appointing him its editor and chief contributor at a reputed £1,500 a year. Lever's editorship wasn't completely real. M'Glashan still held on to the final decision making, and although he let Lever enjoy such trappings of power as presiding over editorial conferences to hammer out ideas and projects, he himself being uncreative, his sometimes crude interference provoked protest. Although Lever wrote four serialised novels for the magazine during his term as editor (1842-45), M'Glashan wasn't satisfied that he was getting enough work out of Lever. He had already urged the author not to live in town where there were too many distractions and temptations. He made Lever live first in Kingstown, but because the new train service made it too easy for Lever to nip into Dublin, he arranged for him to move out to the trainless Templeogue, five miles from the city, there to dwell in what was left of a medieval mansion, once a home of the Knights Templars and later a country seat of the Domvilles, an influential landowning family. M'Glashan was banking on the isolation, dullness and boredom to drive Lever in desperation to work. But such reminders of ancient grandeur at Templeogue House as an artificial waterfall, large paddocks and extensive stabling, incited Lever to acquire twelve horses, which he used to carry himself and his daughters on frolic jaunts around the Dublin hills, and to invite his friends out for stopover visits filled with roistering and card playing.

M'Glashan, in the rôle of guest, started visits of inspection, but these hadn't the intended effect because he seems to have got drunker quicker than the others. It so happens that off the diningroom in Templeogue House there is a small turret room which served as a pantry. One night a footless M'Glashan staggered into this pantry, slamming the door after him and trying to clamber up the shelves in the belief that he was going up to bed.

The easygoing Lever got on reasonably well with M'Glashan, probably regarding his crudities with amused contempt. But in 1845 he gave up the editorship and departed for Brussels, creating a rumour that he was fleeing from creditors. But there's no record of the kind of debt that would force a man like Lever into flight. He probably did live up to the uttermost limits of his income but his departure was probably inspired less by a need to fly from creditors than by a desire to get away from M'Glashan's nagging and nursemaiding, and from a way of life which, as a man entering his fortieth year, he realised was getting him nowhere. He settled future terms with M'Glashan: £50 per sheet for original articles and £10 for reviews, and departed, not for London as Thackeray had urged him, but for mainland Europe. Dublin knew him no more except for a few sentimental visits, and he died, Britain's consul at Trieste, in 1872, more honoured abroad than ever at home.

M'Glashan and the *DUM* continued much as before for some years. But his heavy drinking and prematurely hardening arteries were taking their toll, and in 1856, mistakenly believing that he was on the brink of bankruptcy, he sold his stock, copyrights and recently acquired premises, 50 Upper Sackville Street, to a rising rival, Michael Henry Gill. Gill, Dublin with an Offaly background, was as canny as any Scotsman. Knowing the value of the M'Glashan name, he included it in the name he now traded under, and M'Glashan & Gill was retained as his imprint for twenty years until the firm was re-styled M. H. Gill & Son, making it conform with reality. More than a century later the firm still flourishes, latterly as Gill and Macmillan, doyen and most distinguished of Irish publishing houses.

Earlier I mentioned two chapmen who struck it lucky. James Duffy and Luke White both moved from the bag-on-back end of the business to printing and publishing. In Duffy's case the cobbler stuck proudly to his last. Duffy's became one of Dublin's longest established publishing firms, specialising in the word of God and wholesome plays and novels. Duffy's didn't change with the times, however, and a long and honourable career dwindled into nothingness in the 1970s.

Luke White abandoned bookselling and became a landed gentleman, his grandson becoming a peer of the realm. Just how Luke managed to accumulate so much money has remained a puzzle. Legend whispers that he found a book he had bought in a job lot hollowed out and stuffed with banknotes. It must have been some volume, and the notes of very large denomination, if they enabled him to buy Luttrellstown Castle and its estate from the Earl of Carhampton and to live there at a level of grandeur that had beggared the earl. A condition of sale of Luttrellstown Castle was that its name be changed. Luke White accordingly called the place Woodlands, and as such it became an Irish seat of the family when they were ennobled as Barons Annally of Annally and Rathcline, Co. Longford (1863). But in 1891 the reigning Lord Annally restored the ancient name, and the place has remained Luttrellstown Castle ever since.

Luke's own origin is as mysterious as his fortune's. According to his tombstone in Clonsilla church he was born in 1752. Where isn't mentioned. Legend again whispers that he was a Manxman who arrived in Dublin without a penny to make his fortune.

He is supposed to have called to a bookseller's where an assistant had been advertised for, and found that the bookseller was out visiting a friend. He followed him, but slipped on the pavement outside the friend's house and twisted his ankle. He was taken in and allowed to remain until the ankle healed, when the bookseller gave him the job and eventually made him his heir.

One of Luke White's sidelines was an agency for a London finance house connected with the state lottery. One day Luke found himself with unsold tickets which it was too late to return. He resigned himself to a £60 loss — but one of the tickets won the £20,000 prize. Before long Luke was able to organise a syndicate to loan the government money, having a grateful lord lieutenant honouring him with a visit to a garden party. The former door-to-door book salesman ended up a Member of Parliament as well as a landed gentleman whose posterity married into titled families and eventually became related through marriage to the British royal family.

9

DEVELOPING THE SUBURBS

1

AT some point in its history a large tract of land on the northern side of Dublin Bay was in the possession of a bull so remarkable for something or other that the whole area was designated the bull's meadow, Cluain Tarbh in Irish, a name in due course englished as Clontarf. John D'Alton in his *History of the County of Dublin* (p. 70) says the bull's meadow, or plain of the bull, got its name from 'the fanciful appearance of the large sandbank in front of it, and which still retains the appellation in the English tongue.' A famous battle between Danes and Irish was fought there in 1014 which, like many another famous battle, didn't settle anything but left Dublin still Danish and the surviving residents of Clontarf free to pick up the threads again when the raping and the looting had petered out. A somewhat more far reaching change occurred nearly two centuries later when a Norman invader handed over Clontarf and district to a hanger-on whose name was spelt Adam de Feipo until the wonders wrought by Irish education changed it to Phepoe.

Phepoe's lands presently fell into the possession of the Grand Priors of Kilmainham who vied with the monks of St Mary's Abbey in piling up more treasures upon earth than in heaven. In due course the Grand Priors were helped on their way out of Kilmainham by the monastery-dissolving Henry VIII, and their Clontarf property, after a brief stay with a Cromwellian, was bought by the Vernon family about 1660. It remained with them for three centuries. The Vernons lived in Phepoe's castle, proudly inscribing the family motto over the entrance: *Vernon semper viret* (Vernon always flourishes). They ensured the flourishing by appropriating everything they could around Clontarf. In the early eighteenth century they had a row with the Corporation about a tract of strand described by them as 'the Pool and Island at Clontarf', a row which like the earlier battle settled nothing. But they were able to live in their castle, snug in the possession of nearly a thousand acres of valuable land on the city outskirts, until the building became unsafe in the 1830s. It was replaced by the present mock-Gothic structure designed by the Clonmel-born architect William Vetruvius Morrison.

The Vernons let most of their land in building lots at a rent of £10 an acre, land not suitable for building going at £7, and cabins without land being available at £4 to £5 a year. The building of the Dublin to Drogheda railway, which had a station at Clontarf, developed the possibilities of the place as a dormitory suburb combining convenience to the city with the advantages of a seaside resort. Until well into the present century it could be said that 'the green lanes of Clontarf are justly celebrated for their sylvan beauty,' this being partly because of the several large country houses and their pleasure grounds.

The most historic was Marino, built in the middle of the eighteenth century by a prosperous linen manufacturer, Thomas Adderley, who had married the widowed Lady Charlemont and intended the house to be a gift for his stepson, the future 'Volunteer Earl', whom he greatly liked. Lord Charlemont fell in love with Marino, probably for its views of the bay and of the Wicklow hills in the distance. Marino was itself a plain Georgian block, the rooms small by country house standards of the time, but it did have a sixty foot long art gallery and a fine diningroom with windows of stained glass reputed to be the work of Jervas. The northern wing, which contained the diningroom, was destroyed by fire in 1807, six years after Lord Charlemont's death.

Charlemont, whose family estate was chiefly in Co. Armagh, had little liking for the North of Ireland, having been born and bred in Dublin. In youth he made an unusually prolonged grand tour, then settled in London as an absentee landlord, where he became one of Dr Johnson's circle. In early middle age he became converted to the view that 'it was my indispensable duty to live in Ireland, and I determined, by some means or other, to attach myself to my native land and, principally with this view, I began those improvements at Marino, as without some attractive employment I doubted whether I should have resolution to become a resident.' Regarding residence in Ireland as 'the first of political duties' Charlemont went on to declare that Ireland could never be served in England and confessed that had he settled in London:

> he would soon be tempted to affect to deride his native manners and partialities. The Irishman in London, long before he has lost his brogue, loses or casts away all Irish ideas, and, from a natural wish to obtain the goodwill of those with whom he associates, becomes in effect, a partial Englishman. Perhaps more partial than the English themselves.

Lord Charlemont's summary was that 'Ireland must be served in Ireland. The man who lives out of his country is guilty of a perpetual crime.' The improvements at Marino which were to create the bond between its proprietor and his native land included the enlargement of the house by the addition of wings, and the planting of the 200 acres he acquired on a long lease from the Corporation with trees and rare shrubs.

There was also a folly called Rosamund's Bower, a ruined temple, the *sine qua non* of any eighteenth-century pleasure grounds and, most famous of all, the Casino.

We don't know precisely why Charlemont built the Casino. It would have been partly to gratify the passion for building that he developed around this time, especially a building of breathtaking beauty. But it must also have been to provide himself with a refuge from family life. For he was one of nature's bachelors and had married, it's said, only because when showing his younger brother and heir presumptive how well the trees were growing at Marino, the brother recklessly remarked that when the property came to him he'd cut all those trees down and sell them for timber. Charlemont said nothing at the time but resolved to provide himself with a legitimate heir who he would rear to love and cherish Marino and its beauties. He accordingly proposed to a Miss Mary Hickman from the Co. Clare, a girl of little fortune but diplomatic enough to accept without demur his sledgehammer hints that he was set in his middle-aged ways and wasn't going to change them for any woman and that her rôle would be to provide for the succession.

It's pleasing to be able to record that the marriage turned into a comfortable and affectionate relationship, Mary Hickman keeping her part of the bargain by providing two male heirs. She also kept open house at their two Dublin homes for her Co. Clare relations, so that Charlemont House in Palace Row (now the Hugh Lane Art Gallery, neé Municipal Gallery of Modern Art in Parnell Square) and Marino were nicknamed the Hickman Hotel. In these circumstances it isn't surprising that Charlemont made the Casino not only decorative but practical. It is a self-contained dwelling, entirely adequate to the needs of a rich cultured finicky bachelor: on the principal storey a vestibule, saloon, study and boudoir; a bedroom upstairs and kitchens and wine cellars in the basement, with lions on pedestals at each of the four corners of the building as vigorous symbolic guardians of the privacy of the owner within.

Externally the Casino is a miracle of exquisite stonework: sculptured architecture. Internally it's a connoisseur's paradise: floors of inlaid wood of various colours, the doors mahogany at one side and cedar at the other, both empanelled, the mouldings richly carved. The architect, Sir William Chambers, was never to set eyes on the Casino. He contributed his part in the creation of a masterpiece per post, as he did with the Charlemont town house, which was chiefly used for formal entertainments and as a private museum and art gallery filled with the spoils of Italy, and what for bibliophiles would be a mouthwatering library.

The eighteenth century admired the Casino. The nineteenth, speaking through John D'Alton the historian, felt 'it might be thought too laboured in its embellishments'. Today it is so revered that the Board of Works has spent a fortune restoring and renovating it after the damage it suffered while in the care of the Christian Brothers.

The preferred home of Lord Charlemont's son and heir, who lived to be eighty-nine (his wife made ninety-five) was Roxborough in Co. Tyrone, but he maintained both the Dublin houses on an income that really wasn't adequate for such a lifestyle, his father having fatally weakened the family fortunes by building them. His nephew, who succeeded in 1864, promptly sold the library at Charlemont House, removed the doors and several of the mantelpieces to Roxborough, and in 1870 sold the building to the government to be used for the General Registry. Since neither of his two wives produced offspring, he felt free to spend his patrimony without thought for the future. Percy Fitzgerald in his anonymously published *Recollections of Dublin Castle & of Dublin Society* gives a sketch of them and their way of life which could be applied to many others of the class and time:

The pair lived a jocund, expensive life — certainly beyond their means — after the then fashion of Irish nobility. They had a good old house in the north, but built a new chateau on modern lines — which must have been the last straw. They were also seen much in London during the season, taking a house in a fashionable quarter and entertaining a good deal. Gradually the fine old objects of art, such as the Hogarth pictures — painted specially for Dr Johnson's Earl — the notable 'Peg Woffington' . . . furniture, &c., began to melt away. I remember an eminent Bond Street dealer being on a visit at their house — a most gentlemanly personage, treated quite as an honoured guest; no doubt he was combining business with pleasure.

Eventually Marino itself was given up and the Countess of Howth moved in. Lady Howth, having endured a quarter of a century of married life at Howth Castle, left her husband there and spent the rest of her days flitting between Marino and a house in Merrion Square, with mansions in London and in Hampshire to vary the monotony. When she died in 1884, the Christian Brothers took over and the decline of Marino as a haven of beauty was accelerated. The lease of most of the lands fell in 1921, the house was knocked down and Dublin's concrete jungle was extended to take in the southern part of Charlemont's pleasure grounds. The Casino was for some strange reason left standing, but its roofing lead was pilfered, the weather rotted the exposed timbers and the place might soon have tumbled down altogether if it hadn't been made a national monument in 1930 and temporary repairs carried out on the roof. Today the concrete jungle has crept nearer and nearer, and Dublin Corporation would have let houses be built right up to the Casino's very steps had an elitist row not been kicked up and had the International Architectural Heritage Year not been made the excuse for restoring it to glory behind a tall wire fence in the middle of an attenuated site.

Many of Clontarf's other stately homes have inevitably come to grief. Donnycarney House, once the country home of Alex Thom of the directories, is a golf club. Beaumont, rural refuge of a brewery Guinness, is swallowed up in a hospital complex. Clontarf Castle is a hotel. And St Anne's, the Italianate palace of a later Guinness, has vanished altogether.

St Anne's was the grandest of the stately homes. It was acquired

135

and enlarged in the middle of the nineteenth century by Sir Benjamin Lee Guinness: dapper, pious, spruce, genial and an efficient enough administrator to put the brewery on the path to commercial greatness and channel enough of its profits into his own pocket to make himself Ireland's first real millionaire. Originally called Blackbush, Guinness renamed it St Anne's, perhaps in compliment to his only daughter Anne, who married a clergyman of lordly stock, whom Guinness promptly launched on the path of preferment leading to the archbishopric of Dublin.

Guinness acquired more land around St Anne's, and had the place in excellent shape when bequeathing it, together with half the brewery, to his eldest son.

This son, later Lord Ardilaun, had married a daughter of the Earl of Bantry, a sprig of recent aristocracy, who nagged at him to get out of trade and be a gentleman. After five years of nagging she got her way. Lord Ardilaun, as we shall call him for the sake of convenience, sold his share in the brewery to his younger brother for £680,000. Freed from the taint and the inconvenience of commerce, he started a new career as an almost full-time do-gooder. He completed the exterior renovation of Marsh's Library, begun by his father, altering it beyond recognition. He repaired St Patrick's Deanery, rebuilt the Coombe Lying-In Hospital, chivvied the government into founding the Science and Art Museum in Kildare Street, financed (with his brother) the Great Dublin Exhibition of 1872, the permanent buildings of which later became University College Dublin and, later still, the National Concert Hall. He also rescued St Stephen's Green from private ownership and turned it from drab flat greensward into the pleasing landscaped public park it still is. He took his title of Ardilaun from an island in Lough Corrib, on the banks of which he enlarged a small Georgian country house into a mock medieval castle (now a hotel) which looks more authentic than Windsor. Lord Ardilaun now sits in bronze in St Stephen's Green, one of the few survivors of the IRA purge of statues there, gazing in the direction of Guinness's brewery and, ever regardful of the public need, with a Ladies and a Gents at his right hand.

Such was the cold, kindly, aloof man who, encouraged by his wife, transformed St Anne's from a conventional four-square Georgian house into a palazzo, facing it with limestone meticulously carved, providing it with a marble grand staircase lined with marble columns, a marble ballroom, and loos of marble and mahogany. The grounds were to match.

Like others of his class and religious persuasion he lived in constant fear that the Church of Ireland, disestablished by Gladstone in 1869 — plundered, robbed, murdered were preferred descriptions — would be subverted by the Scarlet Woman of Rome. As defensive measures he paid half the cost of maintaining the choir of St Patrick's Cathedral, acquired the Dublin *Daily Express* and the *Evening Mail* for a while so that the threatened faith could have a morning and evening mouthpiece, and finally built a church at the bottom of his garden at St Anne's, so that no matter what happened in the city, his Church of All Saints at Raheny would save the area from outer darkness. The final touch was to provide himself with a hygienic and well lit vault at All Saints.

After his death, his widow lived on at St Anne's and at Ashford. She continued her husband's benevolence on a somewhat reduced scale, inviting distressed gentlewomen to afternoon tea and presenting each with a potted geranium as they left. From her the Ardilaun property passed to a nephew, a bishop with advancing teeth and a receding chin, from whom it passed to Dublin Corporation. During the war years (1939-45) it was loaned to the army which, in accordance with well-established military precedent, burned it down accidentally. Roofless but still eminently respectable, it survived in a structural condition resembling that of the distressed gentlewomen who used to have tea there, until a Corporation demolition squad arrived to put it out of its misery during the 1960s.

Inevitably, the story of St Anne's echoes the story of other mansions in the Dublin area. The charming red brick Santry House was another victim of military spontaneous combustion. Drumcondra House is now a seminary, but was once the home of an eighteenth-century judge, Sir Marmaduke Coghill, a bachelor who advised husbands whose marriages were endangered to beat their wives — but in moderation, and with a stick of no greater thickness than their thumb. The other elegant classical mansion not far away, Belvedere, is now a teachers' training college under the name St Patrick's. Aldborough House, at the Five Lamps, the last great classical town house to be put up in Dublin, was in turn a school and a barracks, until it attained its present rôle of post office depot. In almost every case the park-

137

lands of these houses have been built over in haphazard way, the use of the space being governed by contractors' greed, sanctioned by Dublin Corporation, with no thought for public amenities.

The Phoenix Park itself might now be a housing estate or an industrial complex if Charles II's rapacious mistress the Duchess of Cleveland had managed to get her hands on it. The land had once formed part of the extensive holdings of the Knights Hospitallers of Kilmainham, and from 1618 contained a viceregal residence of sorts. The Park as such began to come into existence in the 1660s when the viceroy, the relatively public spirited Duke of Ormonde, bought up on the crown's behalf enough land around the viceregal residence to form a deerpark. To the Hospitallers' 400 acres he added another 400 bought from the Lord Chancellor, Sir Maurice Eustace. Then another 100 acres were acquired, and the holding was built up until the new Park extended to 2,000 acres. An area at Kilmainham was handed over to the new Royal Hospital there, which really was as much a palace for the commander of the forces in Ireland as a home for old soldiers.

The Duchess of Cleveland got to hear about this desirable piece of crown property and soon wheedled it out of the king. The patent was made out and actually ready for signing when Ormonde was told of what was happening and put a spanner in the works. He and the next viceroy, Lord Capel, did the same thing a few years later when the Duchess of Cleveland's successor in Charles's favour, the Duchess of Portsmouth, had a try for the Park. But the ease with which Charles appears first to have been parted from his park only to follow this with his reluctance to sign the patent, suggests that he allowed the one to avoid hassle with the women and the other to retain what he never had any real intention of parting with, thus keeping in with both sides. This would have been characteristic of Good King Charles.

At any rate the Park's 1,752 acres were preserved for the public enjoyment, save for the pleasure grounds allocated to the official residences there of the viceroy (now Aras an Uachtarain), the Chief Secretary (now the American Embassy), and the Ulster Secretary (for many years the Papal Nunciature, now in limbo awaiting a decision on its badly needed restoration). There was also the Ranger's Residence, now the Ordnance Survey).

Dublin was also fortunate in certain other projects, this time successful, in which the development of the land was orderly and graceful, and care was taken to provide proper amenities. Needless to say, these projects were for the rich. One, on the city's north side, was carried out by the Gardiners; another, on the south side, was the work of the Fitzwilliams.

2

When Dublin first began to take on its present shape, just over two hundred years ago, it looked as if the north side would always be the more fashionable one. It had the traditional advantage of rising ground, and prosperity prefers to dwell on an eminence. The Gardiner family accordingly bought up as much as they could of the north Dublin hillocks, the area now covered by Mountjoy Square and Summerhill. The first Gardiner purchaser, and founder of the dynasty, was named Luke. He is supposed to have begun his career as footman to a banker and by eavesdropping on his master's conversations picked up useful financial tips which he turned to good account. His gains enabled him to go into banking on his own account, in partnership with one of the Hills of Hillsborough, Co. Down. While there may be some truth in this version of the family's rise in the world, it's more probable that Luke Gardiner was the natural son of some nobleman who settled a small capital sum on him to help him get a good start on the ladder. Such a good connection, even if irregular, would explain how he was able to marry a granddaughter of a Northern magnate, Lord Mountjoy. When the Mountjoys died out and Luke's descendants were offered a peerage in their own right, they revived the title for their own use.

Among Luke Gardiner's earlier acquisitions was land in the Sir John Rogerson's Quay area, where presently one of the streets was named with discreet ambiguity after Saint Luke. A couple of years later he bought property on the north bank of the Liffey from Henry Moore, Earl of Drogheda, who less discreetly had bestowed each component of his name and title on some street in the area (Henry Street, Moore Street, Earl Street and so on, even to an Of Lane. The Drogheda thoroughfare became Sackville Street/O'Connell Street.)

Luke continued to buy land in this area and in the 1720s launched his first major development, Henrietta Street, the most majestic street of its size in these islands. Luke employed the German immigrant Richard Castle, architect of Leinster House and other famous mansions, to design some of the Henrietta Street houses. One, No. 10, became Luke's own town house. His country house (or rather one of them) was only a couple of miles away in the Phoenix Park, Luke having abused his position as Park Ranger to appropriate part of this public property for himself and put up Mountjoy House, now part of the Ordnance Survey and sadly changed. Luke was interested in amateur theatricals, and had a large private theatre included in the building. You can still get into it because it survives as a much partitioned public office.

Luke put his theatrical interests to good use. In 1736 he got himself made Master of the Revels to the Viceroy, worming his way further into high society by procuring a seat on the Privy Council. As a Councillor he was chosen to head the commission of inquiry into Swift's alleged madness. The finding was that Swift was indeed of unsound mind and not capable of taking care of his person or fortune. I note with regret that one of the jury who so lamentably mistook the effects of a stroke for insanity was named Donovan.

Dublin owes several amenities to Luke Gardiner, not the least being the length and useful breadth of O'Connell Street. When Luke began developing Dublin in the 1720s, the future O'Connell Street was merely part of a cart track leading from the ancient walled city to the rural village of Drumcondra. It was lined with old houses, full of character and atmosphere, one guesses, as well as rats and rising damp. Nevertheless, if early eighteenth-century Dubliners were anything like their late twentieth-century descendants they must have raised quite a Wood Quay outcry when Luke, having acquired these old houses, sent in his demolition squads. He proposed to replace these old-world homes with great staring brick mansions, larger and more grandiose than the traditional dwelling places of the city.

Moreover, these new houses would not be lived in by true Liffeysiders (they couldn't afford them) but by country folk who, thanks to the post-Boyne political tranquillity, no longer found it necessary to crouch in stone towers on their provincial property, ever ready to defend it against raids by the dispossessed former owners. These magnates were now free to come up to Dublin with their womenfolk to enjoy an urban social life

140

centred on viceregal receptions at the Castle and other such pleasures. As they wished to give parties as well as go to them they needed large apartments for receiving and entertaining which in turn called for more elaborate kitchens and sculleries. Stables and coach houses were also needed. In short, the moneyed people were ready for a new-style Dublin house; the situation was ready for a developer like Luke Gardiner, and Luke Gardiner. was energetically ready for the situation.

His Henrietta Street was an essay in early town planning and a triumphantly successful one in every important way. It soon became known as Primates Hill, from the number of bishops who built their town palaces there. Every other house was occupied by a peer of the realm. It was Dublin's Park Lane. Luke Gardiner set out to repeat the success in the future O'Connell Street. The newly cleared section of Drumcondra Lane would be laid out as one of those residential rectangles always called squares, its breadth would be 150 feet from house across to house instead of the old intimate street width of ten or fifteen feet. A forty-eight-foot-wide tree-lined walk would go down the middle and be known as Gardiners Mall. Truly a new look Dublin. And it caught on. The protests of conservationists were in vain. The law and the profits were on Luke Gardiner's side, and his new development was another lucrative success.

Luke's son, Charles, proved the truth of the proposition that talent skips a generation. He was no great shakes as a developer, preferring music. He accepted a doctorate of music from Trinity College in 1764, the same year that the future Duke of Wellington's father got himself appointed the college's first professor of music. When Luke died Charles fell in for his official posts, but did little for the Gardiner property except live off it. He married a Meath girl, begetting three sons and two daughters during the intervals of playing concertos with his friends. In August 1769 his pockets were further filled by the inheritance of the fortune of his kinsman Lord Mountjoy, the last of his line and by then further ennobled as Earl of Blessington.

Perhaps the worry of all that money was too much for a musician. Perhaps it was merely the family tendency to high blood pressure. But three months after coming in for the Blessington windfall, Charles himself died. He was only forty-nine. He bequeathed profitable tracts of Dublin with ready cash to match, to his eldest son Luke the Second.

141

Luke the Second didn't care a hoot about music or drama. His passion was the army but, wanting to run his own military show, he joined the militia and became a colonel right away. When he had drilled his amateur warriors to exhaustion, he changed into civvies and continued developing Dublin along his grandfather's lines. But he was not unfilial. He named one of his developments Great Charles Street in memory of the deceased concerto player.

Scorning to be anything so frivolous as Master of the Revels, the second Luke went for the post of Governor of County Dublin, and in between times created Mountjoy Square, Gardiner Place, Denmark Street, and so on. He was jeered at for his moneygrubbing by the Dublin wags. (*Q*: 'Why is a Gardener the most extraordinary man in the world?' *A*: 'Because no man has more business upon *earth* and he always chooses good *grounds* for what he does. He turns his *thyme* to the best account and raises his *celery* every year etc.')

In spite of his military tastes, as a man of property he had a vested interest in peace. Nothing upsets the property market like civic unrest (as the developer of Foxrock discovered to his cost a century later). So the second Luke, letting it be known that some of his best friends were Catholics, prudently introduced parliamentary measures to relieve the Romans (1778 and 1781). These were only partially carried out but they served as a useful insurance policy for the Gardiner house property.

The second Luke also tried to secure complete civic equality for Catholics. This would have given him the spiritual satisfaction of making a noble gesture and the temporal benefit of making the Romans prosperous enough to lease sites from him. But the Lord Chancellor, Black Jack Fitzgibbon, son of a renegade Catholic, who was making his money out of law not land, therefore felt free to scotch the liberal snake.

Luke had married at the age of 28 Elizabeth Montgomery, one of three daughters of a Scottish baronet who were known as The Three Graces. It was an advantageous match, making him eligible for a peerage. In 1789 he was made a baron, reviving the recently extinguished title of Mountjoy held by his grandmother's family. Six years later he was promoted to Viscount Mountjoy, and in due course might have achieved seventh heaven as Earl of Blessington. But two things were against him. On the death of his wife in childbed at thirty-two he perpetrated a fearsome misalliance by marrying a girl said to have been brought up to the millinery trade. An eighteenth-century peer who married a shopgirl more or less disqualified himself from high society.

The other opposing factor was Fate. In 1798 Luke took up arms in defence of Morality and Property against the onslaught of those menaces to both, the United Irishmen. He led his militia to Wexford and there, at the battle of New Ross, was picked off by a baker's boy sniping from a window.

It took some time to recover his body which had been disgracefully mutilated. As a result he couldn't be ceremonially deposited in the family vault in St Thomas's until 15 June, ten days after his death. (Ironically he did not find rest eternal even there, because St Thomas's was destroyed in 1922, and Luke and his relatives had to be moved up to a vault in St George's, which is of course right in the middle of Gardinerland.)

Luke's son and heir Charles was another case of the Gardiner commercial talent skipping a generation in favour of the artistic. At seventeen years of age this Eton-educated youth succeeded to an estate consisting of 32,274 acres of Co. Tyrone, and, in Dublin city and county, to the Lordship of St Mary's Abbey and Grange of Clonliffe (in other words the Mountjoy Square and Gardiner Street complexes) as well as what is now Benburb Street, George's Quay, Mercer's Dock, Poolbeg Street, North Strand, and Broadstone. The yearly rents from the Dublin properties amounted to £13,322 18s. 6d. Co. Tyrone put a further £10,000 or so into Charles's purse.

To find yourself a millionaire at seventeen isn't good for the soul. The wonder is that Charles turned out merely a good natured spendthrift and not a monster. The Gardiner liking for theatricals effloresced in him into a riotous extravagance in renovating and embellishing houses that brought ruin to the family. The oft-quoted example of his extravagance is his first wife's funeral. This lady, like his mother, died young (twenty-eight) in childbed while providing him with a son and heir. Presumably overcome with grief, gratitude, and the prospect of mounting a glorious funerary spectacle, Charles determined to giver her the wake to end all wakes.

He acquired a famous gold embroidered pall, originally made for a French marshal, and under this had the deceased lady carried from St Germains, where she had died, back to the family

143

drawing-room in Henrietta Street. The apartment was festooned with the richest wax candles. Dublin was freely admitted to view the show, which had been staged by an undertaker brought specially from London who, a kindred Thespian at heart, in the necessary absence of applause kept begging the spectators for verbal reassurance that the production was to their entire satisfaction.

The funeral is believed to have cost Charles the equivalent of £200,000 in modern values.

In spite of the vulgarity of his funeral pageant, it was Charles who achieved the pinnacle of the Gardiners' social glory. In 1816 he was created Earl of Blessington for reasons so unclear that one is driven to suppose that he must have greased somebody's paw. With the longed for coronet secured he felt free to follow in father's footsteps and marry the girl he wanted, although from society's viewpoint she was ineligible. She was the plumply pretty and childless widow, Marguerite Power, formerly of Clonmel, still remembered as the literary lioness of Kensington Gore. Marguerite and Charles made the Gardiner money fly faster than ever, but not much of it flew around Ireland. They divided their time between London and Paris.

An intimate friendship developed between Charles and the effeminately beautiful Count D'Orsay. Lady Blessington fell for D'Orsay too, raising no objection to the way Charles showered Gardiner gold on their joint favourite. But Charles's happiness was clouded by the ill health of his little son, the third Luke Gardiner. At nine years of aged the boy joined his mother in the family vault under St Thomas's Church, leaving Charles without a legitimate heir to his estate and title.

Charles now did rather an odd thing. Upset by what he called 'the uncertainty of life', or perhaps at Lady Blessington's suggestion, he altered his will, bequeathing the Dublin property to D'Orsay but subject to the payment of £3,000 a year to Lady Blessington. One would have expected Lady Blessington to get the lot, or at least a life interest in it. But she may have persuaded her not very strong minded spouse that making D'Orsay the heir was the surest way to keep that gorgeous butterfly where they both wanted him.

The altered will also tells us that Charles planned to marry his legitimate daughter Harriet, then aged ten, to D'Orsay, then aged twenty-two.

All in all it is hard to resist seeing in the will the delicate and farsighted scheming of the girl from Clonmel. Not alone did it ensure for her and her husband the continued intimacy of the gorgeous one, but his inauguration as prospective son-in-law provided a neat cover for an ambisextrous *menage*. A cover up was very necessary. Only a few months previously a great scandal had been raised when the Bishop of Clogher was caught *in flagrante* with a soldier. (The bishop promptly disappeared and resurfaced in Scotland as a barman.) Shortly afterwards the British Foreign Secretary, Lord Londonderry, better known to us as Lord Castlereagh, fell under similar suspicion and disappeared into a tomb in Westminster Abbey after slitting his throat. But Charles's intimate regard for a beautiful youth need cause no raised eyebrows when that youth was his designated son-in-law.

But all human relationships are subject to change. Something happened in the *menage*. Charles presently made a new will in which the Dublin property was bequeathed to Harriet herself, provided she married D'Orsay, the Tyrone land went to the illegitimate children, and Lady Blessington's legacy was reduced from £3,000 a year to £2,000.

Whether Lady Blessington actually knew the terms of the new will or not is uncertain. But she seems to have developed doubts about the reliability of her easily influenced husband because four years later she was party to an extraordinary transaction. The fourteen-year old Harriet was actually married off to D'Orsay, bringing him a dowry of £40,000, half in ready cash and half payable a year after Charles's demise. (Charles appeared in excellent health at the time.) Lady Blessington stipulated that the marriage should not be consummated until Harriet was eighteen. Whether it was ever consummated, or whether D'Orsay was even capable of consummating it, was doubted by those who knew him. D'Orsay himself boasted that he left his bride seething in virginity.

The *menage à trois*, now turned *menage à quatre*, waltzed along luxuriously, but gradually the horizon began to darken. At fourteen Harriet might be docile but she soon would be harder to push around. Charles solved the problem before it became serious by falling dead off his horse in a Paris street, a victim of the family malady, high blood pressure. Like his grandpaternal namesake, he was forty-nine. His return to Dublin wasn't any-

145

thing as splendid as his first wife's had been fifteen years before. No disconsolate Lady Blessington and D'Orsay followed his bier. They despatched it to the family vault, unaccompanied.

On paper the *menage* remained rich. Did not Harriet own a large chunk of Dublin? But her trustees discovered that Charles had hocked the property to the hilt and that it was hard to lay hands on much ready cash. What remained available was insouciantly blown by Lady Blessington and D'Orsay, he on clothes and carriages, she on preparations to conquer London high society.

Then the bubble burst. Harriet at eighteen was no longer prepared to suffer the humiliation of playing second fiddle to her stepmother in what should have been her own home, and to be ballyragged around London by her husband as the virgin wife. She fled and sought refuge with her Gardiner relations. A lawsuit over Charles's will was launched against Lady Blessington and D'Orsay, but they just went on living it up in London on money they hadn't got until the bailiffs moved in and they had to flee back to France.

Harriet was to prove herself her father's daughter in the matter of raising mortgages, but these were probably her only means of getting an income out of her heavily encumbered inheritance. Sizeable chunks of the property had to be sold in the late 1840s through the Encumbered Estates Court, perhaps to see her through the several love affairs she had embarked upon.

Harriet's last fling was with Lord Cowper's son, the Hon. Charles Spencer Cowper, original owner of Sandringham, the British royal family's personal estate in Norfolk. She was four years older than he, but they were faithful to each other in their fashion, and when D'Orsay died in 1852 (in an armchair while listening to a waltz) they married.

Harriet, like the rest of the Gardiners, wasn't to comb a grey head. She died at fifty-six in 1869, and so ended the direct link between Luke Gardiner's development and his descendants. For £120,000 Harriet's widower bought what was left of the Gardiner property in Dublin through the Encumbered Estates Court.

3

It didn't take long for the other big Dublin landowning family, the Fitzwilliams of Merrion, to join the new development movement. They were to do for Dublin's south side what the Gardiners had done for the other side of the river. They were less imaginative than the two enterprising Luke Gardiners, but by attracting less attention they also attracted less envy and resentment disguised as admiration, and, making few mistakes, lasted longer.

The Fitzwilliams had settled in Ireland in the thirteenth century, acquiring land here there and everywhere but principally in Counties Dublin and Wicklow. (Their huge Wicklow estate, Coolattin, remained in their possession until the death of Olive Countess Fitzwilliam a few years ago, when it was sold to some native developers.) You can get an idea of the extent of their Dublin property by tracing a line on a map from Trinity College to St Stephen's Green to Kilmacud to Blackrock and back along the coast to the college. The enclosed area was owned by the Fitzwilliams, and much of it still remains the property of their descendants in the female line, the Earls of Pembroke.

It was part of the deep-rooted Fitzwilliam conservatism that they should have remained Catholics long after most other landowners had brought their theological views into harmony with the political situation. Not alone did they fear God but doggedly continued to honour the king even when the king was Charles I and obviously a bad bet. Charles returned the compliment by making the reigning Fitzwilliam, Thomas, Knight of Merrion, Viscount Fitzwilliam. When Charles's troubles worsened and his need of friends increased, he advanced the new viscount to an earldom. But as the Cromwellians happened to have seized the Great Seal of England, it couldn't be affixed to the patent, so Thomas was never legally an earl.

However Charles II settled his father's debts of honour and, a couple of years after the Restoration, created Thomas's son an earl in proper form. But the new earl died without an heir of his body, the title died with him, and only the established viscounty survived. It was extinguished when the childless eighth viscount, last of his line, died in 1833.

The changeover from Catholic to Protestant was made by the fifth viscount, the man who built Mount Merrion House c. 1711, enclosing about a hundred acres as a deerpark and equipping the house with large stables. It was his son, the sixth viscount, born the same year as Mount Merrion House, who at the age of forty took his cue from Luke Gardiner and began the develop-

147

ment which launched the Fitzwilliams along the path to multi-millionairedom.

It might be truer to say it was the viscount's Irish agent who made the move because the viscount, preferring life in England, was an absentee. However when he realised that his Dublin property was a licence to print money he decided to keep a closer personal watch on it. He had Mount Merrion House repaired and renovated, planning to spend much more time there.

The sixth viscount named his first Dublin development after the family estate, Upper Merrion Street. All its houses were handsome but in size and splendour the one built for the Earl of Antrim was the match of anything on the Gardiner property. This house, now numbered 24, is remarkable not only in itself but also as the birthplace of the Duke of Wellington, whose father ruined himself by trying to maintain it in the manner it was accustomed to on an insecure income of less than £8,000 a year. The Land Commission now occupies the mansion, which could well serve as Dublin's No. 10 Downing Street. The union of 1800 more or less finished it off as a gentleman's residence. Lord Cloncurry's memoirs tell us that the house, which had been bought by his father in 1791 for £8,000, was sold ten years later for only £2,500. 'Although still in the best and most fashionable quarter of Dublin,' wrote Cloncurry in 1849, 'it would not now, in all probability, fetch the odd £500.'

But the wheel has turned full circle. Today, if put on the market, No. 24 Upper Merrion Street would surely fetch a million.

To return to the sixth Viscount Fitzwilliam. He enticed the architect John Ensor away from his work on the Gardiner development, inviting him to design a new residential square to be called Merrion Square. This entailed much more site development than you'd imagine from the layout of the neighbourhood as it appears today. In John Ensor's time the north side of the square (the one along which the buses travel) was so low lying that the waters of the Liffey, when in flood, reached it. Boats could be rowed near what is now Holles Street Hospital.

Merrion Square, and the slightly less imposing Fitzwilliam Square which followed it, were in theory a less desirable area to live in than the Gardiners' Mountjoy Square and Henrietta Street. They weren't like the Mountjoy complex, on an eminence over the city, and were distastefully close to the

148

swampy and nasty smelling Liffey. But the area had one advantage the Mountjovians did not enjoy. Ireland's one and only duke, the Duke of Leinster, was living in Kildare Street, in Leinster House, and his back garden occupied a large part of Merrion Square West. His father, who had built Leinster House in what was then an unfashionable area, rightly boasted that no matter where he built, others would follow. So when the sixth Viscount Fitzwilliam made sites available at the bottom of the ducal garden, these were snapped up and Merrion and Fitzwilliam Squares came into being.

The seventh viscount, who succeeded in 1776, also did well when the surrounding area began to be built on. Like his father he lived chiefly in England, although he also made use of Mount Merrion House and got the artist William Ashford to do a series of paintings and drawings of the place and its grounds. He was known in his relations as Mercury because his restlessness kept him on the move at mercurial speed. It is related of him that on one occasion he whizzed from London to Dublin and back in fourteen days.

Oddly enough, the seventh viscount, the second generation of Fitzwilliam developers was, like the second Gardiner generation, a keen musician. He was very fond of Handel, which was normal enough in eighteenth-century England, but was also interested in French music, which wasn't. He developed a passion for Renaissance music and it is interesting to reflect that part of the profits of his Dublin ground rents went to purchasing what is perhaps the most valuable collection of Elizabethan keyboard music in existence, the Fitzwilliam Virginal Book, now preserved at Cambridge.

Unusually for those times he engaged a Catholic woman as his land agent (a double innovation), allowing her and her husband to live in Mount Merrion House. He also built the Catholic chapel at Booterstown in 1812, allegedly at a cost of £6,000, though half that would be the likelier sum. He is said to have personally supervised the building operations.

The seventh viscount lived and died a bachelor, though he is credited with a Grand Passion in his youth for a Cambridge girl who wouldn't have him. And thereby hang two tales.

The first is that in memory of his Cambridge romance he decided to leave his extremely valuable library and art collection to the university there, together with £100,000 to build a museum to house them. Which he did, and to this day the Fitz-william Museum is one of Cambridge's glories. But it more probably owes its existence less to unrequited love than to the seventh viscount's sentimental memories of his student days.

The other tale tells how he made up his mind as to which of his two English cousins should inherit his Irish property. He invited them to tea with the purpose of forming an opinion of their character. One of them, finding the tea too hot, poured it into his saucer and slurped. The viscount decided the other would make a more suitable heir to Dublin 4 and the Fitzwilliam pro-perty passed in 1816 to George Augustus Herbert, eleventh Earl of Pembroke. It was thenceforward known as the Pembroke Estate.

There *was* an eighth Viscount Fitzwilliam, but he never owned the Irish property. He was the childless younger brother of his predecessor, and to avoid having the property passing to childless heirs twice within a short period, he was passed over and given an annuity to support the dignity of the title. On his death in 1833 the line of Irish Fitzwilliam viscounts ended.

The Earl of Pembroke continued to develop the 2,301 acres of Dublin city and county he had inherited with skill and pru-dence. It was during his reign that handsome villas and terraces of smaller houses began to spring up on the fields between Balls-bridge and Blackrock, the owners punctually paying ground rents to his lordship's unmistakeably Irish agent, Mr Cornelius Sullivan, c/o Mount Merrion House. Since the Catholics had their convenient chapel at Booterstown, Lord Pembroke pro-vided the Protestants with a site off Mount Merrion Avenue in 1821 for a church to serve the newly created parish of Booterstown. He got the building fund going with a donation of £1,000 — merely chickenfeed from the Dublin rent roll. By the mid nineteenth-century the Earls of Pembroke were drawing about £60,000 a year from ground rents. It was like having a million a year in modern values.

They could have doubled their takings if they or their agent had been more wide awake. But they had little incentive. The value of the property went on going up of its own accord. New houses created new ground rents, changes in the use of existing houses, forbidden under the tight Pembroke leases, were per-mitted only if desirable and if an increased ground rent were paid. Mount Merrion itself remained a gentleman's residence, its slopes sacred to flowering shrubs, ponies and deer. It was left to the enterprising son of an auctioneer on the Dublin quays, a Protestant financially backed by the Catholic son of a Dublin attorney and wine merchant, to spot the property goldmine on the other side of Mount Merrion which the earls and their agents were lazily ignoring.

True, the land didn't look very promising. It was rocky and hilly, covered with furze bushes and wild grass, and overrun with foxes and hares. It was called Foxrock and Clonkeen. Lord Pembroke and his agent wouldn't have had far to go to find the owners of this land, for these personages occupied a well-known house on the Pembroke Estate — No. 24 Upper Merrion Street, the mansion Lord Cloncurry thought would hardly fetch £500 in the 1850s. They were the Ecclesiastical Commissioners of the Church of Ireland.

4

Many Dublin developers yielded to the temptation to name their developments after themselves or their womenfolk, or after their home town. The Gardiners, with their Mountjoy and Blessington titles, live on in north side street names. The Fitzwilliams and Herberts, Earls of Pembroke, are amply com-memorated throughout their Dublin property. But in vain will you search Foxrock and Clonkeen for a road bearing the name of the queer genius who developed the area. William Wellington Bentley has passed completely from local memory although coin-cidence had fortuitously embalmed the name of his partner in Foxrock. The partner was named Fox.

The Bentley family saga starts a good way back in Dublin lore, but we need only join it at the period when William Frederick Bentley began to flourish. He was an auctioneer in Bride Street who in 1821 married Ann Butler, a girl from Winterfield, Drum-griffin, Co. Galway. Miss Butler had a brother a captain in the 18th Regiment, whom she seems to have regarded as equal in status to a field-marshal.

The new Mrs Bentley didn't allow her husband to forget that he had raised himself by marrying a Butler. The military con-nection was flaunted when it came to naming the sons. Mark, the future solicitor, got Cumberland for a middle name (after the Bloody Duke). John the prudent, canny and socially correct son, suppressed his middle name, which was probably York,

151

after the Grand old Duke of, who had ten thousand men. William, the family go-getter and future founding father of Foxrock, was named Wellington, gloried in it, and determined to deserve it.

Bentley *père* established himself steadily. He moved his auction rooms to Capel Street where he also ran a pawnbroker's and thriftily let an apartment to a tobacconist. He had another auction room across the river at No. 12 Wood Quay. But his lady wife, mindful of what was due to her as a Butler with a brother a captain in the 18th Regiment, declined to live over the shop. Bentley accordingly took No. 37 Charlemont Street, near the Grand Canal, for a family home.

The picture that emerges of William Frederick Bentley is, then, that of a hardworking small-time business man, living prudently, with little of the tycoon about him. But his sons had inherited from their mother something of the Butler family spirit. They pushed old William Frederick into extending his activities into land agency, rent collecting, insurance, and moneylending. A prestigious office was set up in Grafton Street (No. 110, opposite the Provost's House, afterwards taken over by James H. North & Co.) and the Bentleys moved out to a more fashionable home, Laurel Lodge, Blackrock (demolished in the early 1980 to make way for a shopping centre). Through business they made the acquaintance of a Dublin insurance agent, Edward Fox. In theory there was a bar to close partnership between Bentley and Fox. The Bentleys were Protestant, the Foxes Catholic. This, in nineteenth-century Ireland, would normally have kept the families well apart. But the prospect of making money out of a joint venture is a great promoter of the ecumenical spirit the world over: the lion lies down with the lamb, rat joins forces with terrier, and Irish Protestant discovers Irish Catholic to be a man and a brother after all.

Edward Fox, who also ran a stockbroking business in partnership with his brother Anthony, lived in some state in Glenageary. (His handsome house, Glenageary Hall, was demolished in the 1970s and its grounds built over.) The Fox family had made their pile as lawyers and wine merchants and were well experienced in finance. Edward Fox was genial and hearty, kept open house at Glenageary, and fancied himself as an orator. As his obituary notice said, 'at the half-yearly meetings of some of our local companies his speech, always ornate, and

152

delivered with a certain old-fashioned eloquence, came to be regarded as an interesting and attractive feature of the proceedings.'

Whether it was Edward Fox or William Wellington Bentley who first spotted the potential of Foxrock would be hard to decide. It would be tempting to plump for Fox if it weren't that Foxrock was right under his nose and therefore unlikely to be noticed by him. In the 1850s, from the back windows of Glenageary Hall, he could view the wide open spaces between him and the Dublin hills. The land was mostly scrub, but with oases of cultivated parkland around a few mansions like Burton Hall (residence of Mr Guinness, a cousin of the brewery), Leopardstown House (Lord Castlecoote,) and Cabinteely House, occupied by the Misses Byrne and the family skeleton (their grandmother had committed incest with her brother). As Edward Fox's eye roved over the land rising above Deansgrange and Clonkeen, it might have lighted on the chimneys of Kilmacud Manor, home of W. J. Fitzpatrick, who made his money from tallow and used it to finance his researches into the byways of Dublin history. Not far off were the chimneys of Westbury, luxurious dwelling of Thomas Wilson, Governor of the Bank of Ireland and nicknamed 'the Croesus of Dublin'. Down the road was Redesdale, formerly the home of Sir John Mitford, Lord Chancellor of Ireland, later ennobled as Lord Redesdale, ancestor of the Mitford sisters, who so loved the place that he wept on leaving it when his term of office expired and he had to return to England. Between Westbury and Redesdale was an older house, Parsons Green, some apartments of which were occupied by the needy and seedy owner of heavily mortgaged house property in and around Carlow. His name was Walter Bagenal Gurly.

Gurly's sole claim to fame is that he was the maternal grandfather of Bernard Shaw, but he also may have had a parental function in the development of Foxrock as a highly regarded suburb. The records at the Registry of Deeds reveal that he was involved in business transactions with William Wellington Bentley's brother, John, a solicitor, who handled the legal end of the Bentley development schemes. Perhaps it was he who drew the attention of the Bentleys to the development potential of Foxrock, Stillorgan, and Clonkeen, reminding them of the time honoured advice to speculators: walk out of the city until the

153

houses stop, then buy up the land. Much of the land in question was owned by the Ecclesiastical Commissioners, and Gurly was grandson of the Chancellor of the diocese of Leighlin (which embraces Carlow). So you had the situation of three men in the 1850s, connected by business interests: an auctioneer and estate agent; and insurance agent with knowledge of stockbroking and the money market; and a squireen with some experience of property development. The outcome was that 119 acres, 4 roods and 4 perches of land in Clonkeen were leased in the name of the Bentleys for three lives and 397 years from 25 March 1859, from the Ecclesiastical Commissioners and Richard Whatley, Lord Archbishop of Dublin. The head rent was just £235.

After this William Wellington Bentley begins to emerge as the driving force behind the Foxrock project. He appears to shoulder his brother and Fox aside. As for Gurly, assuming he had contributed something to the scheme, he would probably have been paid off with a fee for services rendered.

5

William Wellington Bentley was now thinking big and aiming high — too big and too high as matters turned out. He advanced rapidly on all sides, leasing more mensal lands from the Commissioners, and, with John, acquired 142 acres 2 roods and 15 perches of Keating's land, better known to Foxrockers as Kilteragh. He soon added Kerrymount to his collection as well as land at Taney, Dundrum and picked up more property at Newcastle in Co. Wicklow. He even bought the family home and other property at Blackrock from his now widowed mother, together with her interest in the auction rooms on the quays. Nor did he allow the outer suburbs to engross his whole attention. In 1861, with John as partner, he leased land at Harold's Cross to William North, a builder and ancestor of the auctioneer, to erect houses to be known as Kenilworth Avenue.

And here it can be mentioned that one of W.W.B.'s shrewdest moves was to cash in on Dublin snobbishness by naming his developments after genteel English areas. Thus Harold's Cross was embellished with Kenilworth, Dundrum got Sydenham, and Foxrock was raised to gentility with roads called Westminster, Brighton and Torquay.

W.W.B. didn't sit for long on his acquisitions. He parcelled out the 505 acres of what he now called the Foxrock Estate into sites for detached villas for sale to speculative builders or to people who wished to build for themselves. Within five years some thirty villas had gone up. In 1860 he sold a house he had built on three acres at Westminster Road to John Stanford McIllwaine of the Bank of Ireland, who named it Stanford House. The price was £800, with a ground rent of £28 p.a. McIlwaine was entitled to a further acre 'at a peppercorn rent' if demanded. Bentley leased four more Foxrock acres to Ulick James Daly of 31 Upper Merrion Street at £10 an acre. A further eight acres, also at £10 an acre, went to Jacob Sparrow to build Cairn Hill on Westminster Road. (Sparrow was a wholesale tailor and shirt-maker.) Eleven acres of the extensive grounds originally belonging to Foxrock Lodge on the Stillorgan Road went to a Dublin builder named William Crow, who had already built several of the houses along the road. For some reason or other the ground rent in this case was only £6 an acre. John Bentley himself took a house, Mount Aventine, on Brighton Road, while W.W.B. lived for a very brief time in Hollymount on Brighton Road. But it's interesting to note that he thought Dundrum a more select area than Foxrock, for he charged £16 an acre for a site at Sydenham Road as against £6 and £10 for Foxrock.

Had W.W.B.'s project gone according to plan he would have become a very rich man. Foxrock was to be a dual-purpose development. Primarily it would be a garden city (here W.W.B. was fifty years ahead of his time), but it was also being developed as a select holiday resort which W.W.B. clearly hoped would supplant Bray as the place where well-heeled Dubliners spent their weekends, or had second homes. Foxrock was advertised as 'renowned for the salubrity of the air', and the Tourists' Hotel was put up, at which Bentley established the Foxrock Club.

The Harcourt Street to Bray railway line ran through Foxrock but there was no station. While William Wellington Bentley was repairing that omission he ran a coach service between Kingstown (Dun Laoghaire) railway station and his hotel to bring his weekenders out on Saturday and deliver them back to Kingstown first thing Monday morning. He got the Post Office to open a Foxrock branch, he built a mart (the super-market of the 1860s: Mart Lane is its memorial), opened a 'pic-nic cottage' in Westminster Road, got the railway company to

155

open a station beside his hotel, and himself built the station house.

Things of the spirit were not neglected. He had a Protestant church opened at Brighton Road (Tulla parish church), the incumbent, the Rev. John Fawcett, being handsomely housed in Kerrymount House.

W.W.B.'s plans and projects deserved to succeed, and succeed they did in the long run. But he ran into a certain amount of trouble because of the increase in the Fenian threat during the early 1860s. The timid became nervous about investing money in property in the outer suburbs, these being vulnerable to attack in the event of serious civil disturbance. An alarming word uttered at a dinner party could cause a run on the banks the following morning, for no rumour catches fire quicker than a rumour about money. Some Irish banks were put right out of business in the 1860s as a result of the uncertainty. This general nervousness may have inhibited people from treating themselves to a Bentley weekend, for his hotel didn't thrive. It certainly prevented the big rush to take up Foxrock sites that Bentley had banked on and needed to keep solvent. (Beatrice Glenavy tells us in her memoirs that even in 1888 Carrickmines was 'a wild lonely place'.) Moreover those who did venture out to Foxrock were more the well-to-do shopkeeping and business class than the professional class who would have made the area fashionable.

John, the shrewd cautious Bentley, seems to have been quicker than W.W.B. to realise that the Foxrock party was over, at least for the moment. He began to disengage himself, mostly at his brother's expense. He appears to have sold as much of his interest in the whole venture as W.W.B. had the ready cash to purchase. W.W.B. had a big liquidity problem.

He had started mortgaging part of the Foxrock lands almost from the beginning, first for £5,000, then in January 1861 for £7,000 and for £4,000 the following year. He was also getting in deep with the banks. In 1864 he mortgaged the Foxrock Estate to the Hibernian Bank, and the following year mortgaged land at Kerrymount, Foxrock, Taney and Newcastle, Co. Wicklow to Anthony Fox, Edward's brother and partner in the insurance business. In April 1865 he was £4,247 12s 0d in the red in the books of the National Bank at Kingstown, and the following October the Union Bank of Ireland (itself shortly to go bust) obtained judgment with costs against him for £205 12s 6d. The

156

relatively small sum involved showed how hard pressed he was for cash. A greater humiliation was inflicted on him the following June when a grocer and wine seller in Lower Charlemont Street took him to court for a miserable £52 and got judgment with costs.

In fact he was so pressed against the wall that the day after the Union Bank had him in court he made over the Foxrock Estate to another brother, the solicitor Mark Cumberland Bentley of Brighton House, Brighton Square, Rathgar.

Meanwhile what had happened to Edward Fox? Like John Bentley, this shrewd gentleman had disengaged himself from any overt connection with the doomed W.W.B., an easy enough operation for Fox as he had always remained in the background. W.W.B.'s credit in the Dublin area was now gone. He had to go further afield for mortgages in 1867. He began the year by hocking Kerrymount and part of Foxrock to Thomas Seymour of Ballymore Castle, Co. Galway and John Henry Brett of Rathkeale, Co. Limerick, but within a fortnight his own brother-in-law and a cousin in Kerry got judgment against him for £667. The end of the year found him mortgaging his last bit of land to the Wicklow County Surveyor. And with that he had shot his bolt. There was nothing left but the bankruptcy court or to disappear. He disappeared, and what happened to him I'm unable to tell you, for I can find no trace of him after 1867.

He may have changed his name, but that would have availed him little as he was too well known in and around the city to hide behind an alias. It's more probable that he left the country. Foxrock in general, and the Tourists' Hotel in particular, were known to the older inhabitants as Bentley's Folly, the assumption being that W.W.B. was huddled miserably in some obscure corner of the world, his face turned to the wall. But I doubt if this was his fate. He wasn't the type to accept defeat. I prefer to think that when at last he saw things weren't working out, he slipped into his pocket a few of those thousands he had been juggling about with in mortgages and overdrafts, to help keep him afloat while in some other part of the world he set about developing another Foxrock.

As for John Bentley, he still had the family auctioneering business on which he had never relaxed his grip. With Foxrock a dirty word as far as he was concerned, he disposed of his home there and took a dignified house on Waterloo Road. He also suf-

157

fered a personal loss: a thirteen-year old son died of scarlatina. This may have made Waterloo Road distasteful to him in its turn for he moved out to the southern suburbs again, taking a house in Glenageary, not far from where Edward Fox lived. He died of a stroke at the home of his son in Monkstown, in October 1906. He was 79. His death notice reminded the public that he was a nephew of the late Captain Butler of the 18th Regiment. He left £15,000, good money for the Dublin of 1906.

Edward Fox expired at Glenageary Hall of cancer of the bladder in 1887 at the age of 74, 'fortified by the rites of the Catholic Church, RIP,' but owing money to Parnell's brother-in-law, a solicitor. (Fox left a mere £899 16s 2d.) He rests in Glasnevin in a grave containing seven other Foxes.

After W.W.B.'s disappearance the Foxrock Estate was acquired by the Benedictines, but the reverend fathers presently moved on and the estate passed into the possession of the Royal Exchange Insurance Company. The great stretch of land which William Wellington Bentley had planned to dot with gentlemen's residences became Leopardstown Racecourse. Why hadn't he thought of *that*, you may ask. Perhaps a racecourse *was* included in those grand schemes of his that never matured.

If he survived his brother John by even a few years he may have learned that by the early twentieth century the Foxrock Estate had been given the seal of social approval, for Sir Horace Plunkett, high priest of the Irish Co-operative Movement and a younger son of Lord Dunsany of Dunsany Castle, Co. Meath, and unquestionably a gentleman living on Old Money, had bought a large site at Foxrock on which he built a dream house, Kilteragh. An architectural monstrosity, said some, with its belfry and multitude of gables, towers and flattened chimney stacks, making it resemble the offspring of a misalliance between a South American monastery and an English manor house. But Sir Horace was visited there by Viscount Powerscourt, and Gurly's grandson, Bernard Shaw, was an honoured and admiring house guest.

In 1922 some persons claiming to be Republican patriots burned Kilteragh down. Sir Horace, understandably affronted, declined to rebuild, but accepted the compensation for malicious damage and went to live in England. But by then Bentley's suburban creation was too well established to suffer any real loss of status.

Postscript

John died unexpectedly at 6 o'clock on Monday 26 August 1985. He had been working up till lunchtime, and *Life by the Liffey* was the major item on his agenda. I remember well the day he finished the first draft: Christmas Eve 1984. He handed it to me for typing. Some time during the Christmas holiday, becoming bored with television, I slipped away and started to type. After a while John discovered what I was doing and he said 'Good God! Is this what you're up to? I thought you had gone out. For heaven's sake leave it, there's no urgency. Come on and sit down and relax.'

'It's great', I said. 'I just want to keep on. I love it.'

'But that's only the first draft', he said.

John's first draft, as he called it, a book of 65,000 words, was handwritten in his well-known distinctive style. He was incapable of scribbling. During 1985 he re-wrote from the typed version. His last letter to Fergal Tobin of Gill & Macmillan was dated 8 July when he told him he was almost there.

A couple of weeks after John's death Fergal wrote to me expressing his sorrow at the loss of a friend and colleague. He mentioned that if at all possible the book should be published in commeration of him. I phoned Fergal and said I didn't think so. There was still work still to be done on it and I wasn't sure that John, being the perfectionist he was, would have liked me to give the go-ahead on something that was not completely finished.

Over the next few weeks I read and re-read the first draft, then the second draft and finally the edited but incomplete version. Then I gave the lot to Fergal for his opinion. I knew that John held him in high esteem, having worked closely with him previously on two books of John's published by G & M in 1983.

Some time later Fergal called out to tell me that G & M would be happy to go ahead with the book as John had left it.

I am aware that John had the final short chapter to write: the one which would gather together all the material covered in the book and place it in its proper context. No one but John knew exactly how he would have done it, so we have left it alone. In a way, *Life by the Liffey* is John's Unfinished Symphony.

Dalkey,
Co. Dublin.
March 1986.

INDEX

161

Melbourne, Lord, 22
Mendicity Institution, 59-60
Mercer, Mrs Mary, 47
Mercer's Hospital, 47
Merrion Square, 148
Merrion Street, 148
Mitford, Sir John, 153
Moira, Earl of, 59-60
Moira House, 59-60
Moore, George, 125
Moore, Henry (Earl of Drogheda), 139
Morgan, Lady, 17
Morrison, William Vetruvius, 132
mortality rates, 21
Mosse, Bartholomew, 49
Mount Jerome cemetery, 86, 91
Mount Merrion House, 147, 149, 150
Mount Venus, 125
Mountjoy House, 140
Mountjoy, Lord, 139, 141
Mountjoy Square, 142, 148-9
Mulligan, John, 56
Municipal Gallery, 86
Municipal Reform Act, 35
Murphy, William Martin, 121-4
Mystics, The, 127

Napier, Joseph, 91-2
Nation, The, 8, 116-17
Newgate Prison, 38, 68
newspapers, 99-104, 107-30
Norbury, Lord, 88
North, William, 154

O'Brien, William Smith, 22, 92
O'Connell, Daniel, 22, 87, 89, 117
O'Connell Street, 2, 32, 139-41
O'Connor, 'Tay-Pay', 118
O'Grady, Judge Standish, 88-9
O'Toole, St Laurence, 15
Ormonde, Duke of, 138
Orrery, Lord, 106-7

Parsons, Richard (Earl of Rosse), 34
Parsons Green, 153
Peel, Sir Robert, 71, 126
Pembroke, Earls of, 147, 150-1
'Pether the Packer', 3-4
philanthropists, 46-60
Phoenix Park, 2, 14, 54, 138, 140
  The Hollow, 80
  Murders, 74, 79
Phoenix Tavern, 33
Pilkington, Letitia, 124-5

plague, 12
Pleasants, Thomas, 50-3
Pleasants Asylum for Female Orphans,
  51-2
Plunket, Rev. William Conyngham, 4
Plunkett, Sir Horace, 158
police, 63-74, 79-82
Police Acts, 63, 66
Ponsonby, Colonel, 34
Poor Laws, 22
poor relief, 21-6
population, 72
Powell, Humphrey, 124
Power, Marguerite (Lady Blessington),
  144-6
Poynings' Law, 28-9
preachers, 40-1
printers, 124-7
Prison Gate Mission, 58
pubs, 64 *see also* taverns

Ranelagh, 12, 41, 52
Redesdale, 153
Rich, Barnaby, 15-16, 28
Richmond Penitentiary, 75
Ringsend, 13
Rose, Sir Hugh, 77
Rose Tavern, 32
Rosse, Lord, 34-5
Rotunda Hospital, 23, 49-50, 115
Royal Dublin Society, 53, 54
Royal Hospital, Kilmainham, 138
Royal Irish Academy, 29
Russell, Thomas, 69
Ryan, Captain, 67-8
Ryan, Desmond, 78

Sackville Club, 36
St Anne's church, 35
St Anne's, Raheny, 135-6
St Audoen's church, 11, 13
St Bride's church, 53, 117
St George, Colonel, 34
St John's church, 61
St Mary Magdalen's Asylum, 58
St Mary's Abbey, 14
St Michael's church, 57
St Michan's church, 34
St Patrick's Cathedral, 4, 137
St Patrick's Hospital, 48
St Patrick's Refuge, 58
St Peter's church, 41, 86
St Stephen's Green, 136
St Stephen's Green Club, 36

St Thomas's church, 143
St Werburgh's church, 17, 48, 64, 71
Santry, Lord, 34-5
Santry House, 137
Sarsfield, Patrick, 15
Saunders News Letter, 119
Scott, John, 'Copperfaced Jack' (Lord
  Clonmell), 84-6, 114-15
Semple, George, 48
Seymour, Thomas, 157
Shaw, George Bernard, 7, 117, 153, 158
Shaw, Captain Eyre Massey, 6
Sheares, John, 69
Sheridan, Thomas, 104
Sirr, Major Henry Charles, 66-71
Somerville, Sir William, 116-17
South Great George's Street hospital, 49
Sparrow, Jacob, 155
Spike Island, 98
Spratt, Father John, 54
Stanford, Charles Villiers, 8, 56
Stanyhurst, Richard, 15
Steevens, Grizel, 46-7
Steevens's Hospital, 47-8
Stephens, James, 72, 75
Stove Tenter House, 51
Strafford, Thomas (Earl of Wentworth),
  31
Strong(e), Katherine, 18-20
Sullivan, Cornelius, 150
Sunday Independent, 122
Swan, Major, 67-8
Swift, Jonathan, 4, 7, 18, 28, 38, 46-8
  insanity of, 140
  and publishers, 101-9 *passim,* 125

taverns, 16, 31-2
Taylor, Alfred S., 97-8
temperence movement, 54-5
Thackeray, William M., 5, 129
Thom, Alexander, 126-7, 135
Thornton, Robert, 99

Tone, Theobald Wolfe, 67
trade guilds, 35-6
trade unions, 123-4, 126-7
Trench, Archbishop Richard Chenevix, 7
Trinity College, 13, 47, 48, 54

United Irishmen, 142
Ussher, Arland, 31

Vernon family, 131-2
Vicars, Sir Arthur, 80
Victoria, Queen, 22, 26-7
Vikings, 1, 20
Volunteer Defence Force, 66-7

weather, 12-14
Wellesley, Sir Arthur (Duke of
  Wellington), 70, 148
Wentworth, Earl of, 31
Wesley, John, 59
Westbury, 153
Whalley, John, 101-2
Whalley's News Letter, 101-2
Whately, Archbishop Richard, 39, 154
White, Luke, 124, 129-30
Whitelaw, James, 24
Whiteside, Judge James, 90-1, 95
whores, 6, 58-9
Wilde, Oscar, 38
Wilson, Thomas, 153
wine, 15
Winetavern Street, 15
workhouses, 22-3
Worsdale, James, 34
Worth, Edward, 48

Yeates, Isaac, 56
Yelverton, Barry (Viscount Avonmore),
  86-7
Young Irelanders, 116-17

Zoological Gardens, 54